THE STRATEGY OF
FINANCIAL PRESSURE

The Strategy of
Financial Pressure

A. T. K. Grant
C.B., C.M.G.

Fellow of Pembroke College, Cambridge

BOOKS
10 East 53d St., New York 10022
(a division of Harper & Row Publishers, Inc.)

Published in the U.S.A. 1973 by
HARPER & ROW PUBLISHERS, INC.
BARNES & NOBLE IMPORT DIVISION

ISBN 06-492514-5

Printed in Great Britain

Contents

finance: (i) when prices are rising, to replenish working capital; (ii) when prices are expected to stop rising, to replace long-term finance the flow of which is being held back by uncertainty about future long-term rates.

choice and substitution determining allocation. The demand for additions to the stock of physical assets will be governed by the return to be got from them as compared with the return forgone from the financial claims which they replace, and this governs the rate of physical investment, on straight Keynesian lines.

Preface

This book is the product of a study of British experience in conditions of fiscal and monetary stringency. On the basis of what has been happening over the last ten years, it attempts to explain how it has come about that we have rising prices and rising unemployment at the same time, and to assess some of the consequences. From this interpretation two points stand out as of immediate relevance. The first is that as we come to expand demand in the U.K. we must be prepared to face and solve a number of serious financing problems if output in its turn is to be allowed to keep pace with rising demand. The second is that particular lines of policy, however right they may appear to be in the abstract, can only be used within limits; outside these limits they reach a reversal point beyond which they have effects the opposite of those intended. Of course there is much else in this complicated story, but whether we regard these two issues as conclusions to be drawn from experience or as hypotheses to be put to the test in the near future (which seems inescapable), they are issues which we cannot afford to ignore.

Financial matters of the kind dealt with here are of serious interest to many, though the focus of interest, and the specialised knowledge which goes with it, will vary considerably from reader to reader. The writer on finance has to keep in mind the diversity of his possible audience. I have tried to set down what I have to say as simply as I can, but the matters dealt with cover considerable ground and from time to time are of some moderate complexity, and I would plead this in self-defence if I am thought guilty in places of over-elaborating the obvious.

Finally there are debts to be acknowledged. The work of which this is part has been made possible by a grant from the Social Science Research Council for the purpose of studying the effects of financial pressure on the U.K. economy. Mr E. W. Davis has himself been working on other aspects of the project; I have had the benefit of full discussion with him, and he has also gone through the final draft. Others among friends and colleagues who have helped me with ideas and by commenting on large parts of the draft are Mr John Luce, Dr A. B. Cramp, Mr Michael Zvegintzov and Mr R. P. Smith. I have also received help and encouragement from Professor Lord Kahn and Mr Michael Posner. There are others also in finance and industry and elsewhere who have contributed greatly, through conversation or discussion, to my understanding of the problems here discussed. But in expressing gratitude for time and assistance given so freely, I must make it clear that I alone am responsible for the views I have set down. Finally I must put on record my thanks to the Department of Applied Economics in Cambridge for the facilities it has provided, and in particular to Mrs Lilian Silk and her typing staff.

Pembroke College, Cambridge   A. T. K. G.
May 1972

CHAPTER ONE

Introduction

This book is the outcome of a project set up to examine the effects of the continuous application of financial pressure on the contemporary U.K. economy, contemporary in this context being taken to meet the later 1960's as they merge into the 1970's. The project began by exploring in two main directions: to see the effects of severe national budgeting and severe credit restriction on users of finance, and on suppliers of finance. We had been having a protracted experience of both fiscal and monetary pressure, and so work went ahead on these lines.*

But it soon became apparent that there were other features – unexpected and inescapable – which demanded urgent attention. The credit restrictions bit deeper and deeper and the budget surpluses became awe-inspiring, but the consequences were not such as could have been intended from a policy of such impeccable ferocity. From the autumn of 1969, when our scrutiny of the policy of financial pressure began, we were faced with the continuing spectacle of rising prices and rising unemployment at one and the same time. The connection (if it was a connection) between financial policy and increasing prices and unemployment barred the way and demanded explanation. With the passage of events it was as if the subject matter had taken charge and dictated the direction of the study.

Accordingly this is an attempt to find a way through an obscure, limited and undeniably important field. The approach here takes

* In this connection see Edward Davis, 'Financial Innovation and the Credit Squeeze', *The Bankers Magazine*, November and December 1970. This deals among other things with the new sources of borrowing, and the development of leasing and lease-back.

three directions: first, an analysis of the forces and institutions at work in the developed economy; second, an examination of the relevant basic statistics, to see how far they are consistent with and can contribute to the explanations and interpretations given; third, an attempt to bring the puzzle together and to show how the different pieces fit in, and the relevant general implications which emerge. These three approaches were pursued simultaneously in the working, but in what follows they are set out in sequence. The lay-out is that the chapter immediately following, ('Pressure, Enterprise and Prices') seek to analyse the position and uncover what was happening. The next chapter ('U.K. Experience 1962–1972; Spending, Profits and Liquidity') looks at the figures. The chapter which follows ('The Scope and Limitations of Financial Action') tries to bring out the practical issues bearing on financial policy. The last chapter ('Finance as a Constraint in the Developed Economy') is a generalised elaboration; it is an attempt to get a co-ordinated view of the forces at work and of the further implications (and can be left aside by those who are mainly concerned with matters of immediate practical relevance).

It is only fair to add something at this stage about the themes which will be encountered in the following pages.

To begin with, monetary constriction cannot be regarded as hitting only at demand. A policy of credit denial in order to moderate consumption spending is also a policy which holds back production spending in those cases where some financial reinforcement is necessary if opportunities for increasing output are to be followed up. This may not matter so much at a time of stagnation – provided there are sufficient devices mitigating the discouragement to investment – but it can become of real significance with the change in tempo which would follow a policy which provided a powerful stimulant to increased demand. Demand rises; if supply is held back by financial stringency just at the moment when a temporarily accelerating increase in working capital is needed to jerk output up, there is an immediate impulse towards increased prices, and an added increase to imports, which will be rising anyway. In short, credit restriction can contribute to inflation when it bears on the output side.

Next, the position as seen from the standpoint of a business undertaking. The managers of a company see their money coming in and going out in various directions after appropriate time intervals. If business is prosperous and increasing, they are laying out credit (you do not get paid at once) and meeting increasing bills for wages (even if wage rates do not rise) regularly every week, and for materials, posibly with some increasing delay. The larger the sales, the more credit you have to give, the more costs you have to meet. (It may come right on the night, but the night might be some time ahead, and you may even do more good business in the meantime.) If you cannot get outside money to see you through, you have to slash avoidable expenses. The most easily avoidable expense is new capital investment – it can be postponed to next year, and so on. That puts the limit on growth. But even if your existing capacity will see you through, increasing wage and material bills may in their turn force you to cut back. This is the penalty of success, and if you still go ahead you risk running out of working capital and suffering the fate of those who fail to pay attention to liquidity.

This is the consequence of credit restriction at a time of rising demand as seen from the supply end. The embarrassment may be temporary; once the sharp increase in demand has slowed down, the money from increased sales should start coming through; the bankers may be helpful; but the risk remains of finding yourself being taken over by your creditors or by others who know the financial embarrassment you are in. You may be wise to hold back, be less ambitious, and (unwillingly) go slow and raise prices instead, even if it means exposing yourself to competitors.

Not that this is the only problem connected with financing; there are others, in particular those arising from changes in price levels. You may think that you know where you are when you see prices rising at an apparently steady rate; the price of finance will have adjusted itself, and even if dear it may be manageable. But the moment that uncertainty comes in and there is a possibility of the price rise slowing down, and perhaps even of some stability in prices, the cost of long-term money becomes forbidding. Borrowers have to borrow on short-term (with a view to refinancing when new long-term rates have settled themselves) but they slow down on their long-term expansion plans. Again output and growth are affected. This will especially be the case where complicated and expensive technological developments are involved; technology and finance are not good mixers in Britain.

But the more immediate problem arising from inflation is that connected with the upward movement in wages. The margins here are very narrow. Wage-earners cannot be expected to concede in normal conditions any reduction in real wages: in anything short of a major crisis they are bound to defend their standard of living. This means that take-home pay must keep up with the rise in the cost of living, and this sets the lower limit. But over and above this wage-earners will expect their share of a national income which is assumed to increase, and if wage settlements are not to induce further price rises they cannot on the average exceed the increase in average productivity. When productivity is increasing very slowly, the margin is exceedingly narrow, and the constant pressure will be to exceed it, thereby setting off more price rises. This in turn leads to pressure on profit margins; the businesses affected can try to offset increased wages by a reduction in their labour force, in order to contain the overall wage bill. Up to a point this may be achieved without a loss of output, through increased productivity. Beyond this point it can only be achieved by a lower output and a loss of profitable business, either because higher prices reduce demand, or because shortage of working capital makes it necessary to reduce the scale of operations. Either way the wage-push pressures bring down employment, in contrast to demand inflation where the flow of increased purchasing power leads to expansion of employment at home (and more imports from abroad).

There still remains the question of the use of policy instruments. To increase indirect taxes means an increase in prices; to increase income tax or deductions means a decrease in take-home pay; to demand payment for facilities previously provided without charge leads to a decrease in spending money. Beyond a certain point all these add up to an increase in prices, to be met by a demand for a compensating increase in money wages. A policy which may be sensible, applied with tact and moderation within carefully observed limits, becomes counter-productive when it seems directly to increase the evil it is supposed to bring to an end. There is a reversal point when any saving which the policy seeks to make is outweighed by the demand for more money which it provokes.

There must always be such a reversal point; the question is to decide where and when it comes.

Or again, measures taken to stimulate exports, whatever form they take, must lead to repercussions if the exports do not come from increased production, but leave a vacuum behind them. The gap will be filled by increased imports or will stimulate rises in prices. The condition which such a policy must satisfy if it is to avoid these consequences is that the rate of expansion in exports should not seriously outrun the expansion in production. Too drastic a movement in exports takes one beyond the reversal point, when the advantages of the increased exports are exceeded by the dislocation in the domestic market. And similar considerations apply to all policy instruments when they are pushed beyond a certain point.

What follows is concerned with the implications of matters such as these.

CHAPTER TWO

Pressure, Enterprise and Prices

1. *Objectives and Policy Instruments*

We are concerned with the nature and consequences of financial pressure as exercised in a developed economy such as that of the U.K.

In practice the need for such pressure arises for one (or both) of two reasons: a continuing rise in the domestic prices and/or a continuing deficit on external account.

In practice also the exercise of such pressure involves a price in the form of a slowing down in economic activity. It can also bring about some fall in employment. (One aims to keep these unfavourable consequences to a minimum.)

The U.K. experience of the six or seven years up to 1971 has not gone as expected. From a balance of payments crisis successfully solved we moved into a phase of accelerating price and wage rises accompanied by growing unemployment, and all this at a time of surpluses and squeezes of uncompromising orthodoxy and unprecedented severity. Even with the pressure removed, the signs of recovery are slow in coming. Moreover the unexpected combination of rising prices and rising unemployment – one would normally associate rising prices and labour *shortage* – is not just a domestic problem; something similar is to be found in other developed countries. Hence the need to look closely at what has been happening.

Financial pressure is thought of as operating through fiscal policy (seen in government revenue raising and spending) and monetary policy (seen in the financing facilities available to business enterprise and the spending public). For purposes of this analysis, however, it will be more convenient to work on the basis of five closely related heads; the fiscal balance; distribution of spending power; credit policy; subsidies and concessions; debt management.

Fiscal Balance. This is the familiar surplus or deficit on government account. To the extent that the authorities are in deficit, they are reinforcing effective demand, and to the extent that they are in surplus they are damping this down. By modifying the size of the surplus or deficit they exercise fiscal control. But there are complications, the most important of which concerns spending power.

Distribution of Spending Power. It is not just a matter of how much money is raised (or is spent) but the way in which it is raised. In theory (to take an extreme hypothesis) a budget outturn could be kept unchanged while the economy is controlled by making the tax system more or less progresive in its impact: shifting the burden on to the poorer sections of the population (thereby reducing consumption) and easing it for the rich (who are likely to add to their savings) if the economy is to be damped down, or easing the burden for the poor and increasing taxes on the rich if it is to be stimulated. But in practice we are concerned with the fact that particular taxes (or economies) lead to specific repercussions. One cannot just consider the overall balance; some attention to its components is called for. Changes in taxation, even if the total revenue to be raised is the same – and all the more so if there are changes in the balance – must bear unequally to the extent to which the taxes affect spending and saving among particular groups in different ways.

Credit Policy. This refers to the scale and conditions on which finance is made available for the business community and the general public, and the policies adopted by the monetary authorities and the financial institutions.

Subsidies and Concessions. Both credit policy and fiscal policy are more effective in so far as they can be tailored to meet particular situations. Without a structure of concessions and alleviations – e.g. to encourage investment or to ease the problems of development areas – the effect of tight budget and credit measures could be – if applied with force – to strangle the weaker parts of the economy while leaving other parts unaffected.

Debt Management. The management of the national debt is usually regarded (along with credit policy) as lying in the field of monetary policy, but it raises particular issues, and it will be convenient to be able to examine it independently.

All five aspects interlock. Budgetary policy cannot be considered apart from its impact on spending groups; credit policy implies the structure of exceptions and added facilities which makes it workable and is tied in with government debt policy; finally, the interaction between fiscal and credit policy is of basic importance, and it is to this that we turn next.

2. The Interaction of Fiscal and Credit Policy

When an economy is over-heating, one looks in the first instance for the pace to be checked by a combination of fiscal policy and credit policy.

By fiscal policy is meant the deliberate fixing of the balance between government spending and revenue raising. An increased surplus (or reduced deficit) on public account implies a decrease (or smaller rate of increase) in (i) the effective demand of the community in general; (ii) the level of profit earned by business undertakings; (iii) the attractiveness for such undertakings of extending the scale of operation (they will want to invest less); (iv) the rate at which money is coming in and the proportion of it available for use in expanding the business (reduced cash flow leaving less to invest). (There will also be repercussions on exports and imports but at this stage we are only concerned with the domestic effects).

This subtraction of purchasing power from consumption will, on the assumption that the spending propensities of the public are unchanged, diffuse itself over time. The extent and pace of the diffusion will determine how far increased government revenues are reflected in decreased consumption by the public, and the speed with which the reductions are made effective. Calculations can be made to throw up a multiplier which will show the proportion – after the process has worked itself out – between the amount which the government is getting in by way of increased revenue (as compared with what it would have been otherwise) and amount by which G.N.P. is reduced as compared with what would have happened otherwise. Increased taxation brings down disposable income and to that extent should slow down expansion of the economy.

By credit policy is meant the changing of the scale and terms on which financial resources are on offer to persons, business undertakings and other prospective users. This involves (as will be seen later) some complicated matters which can perhaps be summed up most conveniently in the proposition that anything which makes givers of credit reduce the volume of credit which they are prepared to give, and/or demand more by way of return, and/or impose more stringent tests on those applying for finance must tend to keep down the use of credit below what it would otherwise have been.

At this point one should note in passing one recurring complication; it is concerned with expectations. The volume of credit passing depends not only on what is being offered but on what is being asked. A change of expectations (for example, the introduction of the prospects of early price increases) will bring forward – as long as there are no strongly deterrent interest increases – credit worthy borrowers who would previously not have come forward, and vice versa. In the course of the argument which follows we shall have to recall this particular qualification, to avoid pressing too far conclusions resting on the assumption of other things remaining unchanged.

We are assuming that both fiscal policy and credit policy restrain effective demand. We begin by asking: are fiscal and credit policy (a) complementary; (b) alternative; (c) conflicting, and in what circumstances. Within what limits, if at all, can we compensate lower taxation with tighter credit or vice versa?

The answer– if one may anticipate – can be summarised as follows. Fiscal and credit policy are complementary rather than alternative, but can come into conflict when the objective is to restrict consumption while stimulating investment. Tighter fiscal policy reduces not only consumption, but the prospects and profits (and in time the credit requirements) of industry. Tighter credit policy discourages borrowing for consumption as a way around fiscal constraints, but in the absence of a tight fiscal policy could have little effect on consumption, although it could have highly adverse effects on production by holding back investment (thereby strengthening rather than weakening an inflationary tendency).

Finally, both credit and fiscal policy canot be treated out of context, and in particular to secure their purpose may have to be accompanied by a range of concessions and alleviations in respect of particular aspects of the economy as soon as they begin to press at all harshly on sensitive points.

To some this answer may prove acceptable without further elaboration. But the matters are of importance, and the argument needs to be set out at greater length. This is because one must be prepared from time to time for strong public pressure for tax concessions, to be accompanied by a compensating tightening in credit restraints. The effect of this could be serious. The arguments are therefore examined – perhaps somewhat laboriously – in the rest of this section on the interaction of fiscal and credit policy.

One begins with the problem in its most elementary form, and takes it in stages. The economy is overheating. We need to control effective demand through fiscal and credit measures.

To see the process at work clearly, we need four simplifying assumptions. First, we take it that we are concerned only with keeping down effective demand in general, and for the moment can ignore the impact on particular types of demand. Second, we assume that there is no difficulty in making the measures effective, by explicitly assuming a constant propensity to consume. Third, timelags are for the moment ignored. Fourthly, we assume that the facts of the situation are as given and that other things continue unchanged: that is, we do not need to trouble ourselves about such matters as spontaneous changes in expectations (from within) or interruptions (from without). These drastic assumptions have to be removed later.

On the basis of these assumptions the situations can be set out as follows.

Case 1: expanding effective demand checked by tighter fiscal measures; credit terms unchanged. The increased government surplus (or reduced deficit) leaves people with less income to spend. (a) Demand is reduced below the level which it would otherwise have reached, assuming an unchanged marginal propensity to consume. However (b) consumption spending may to some extent be sustained by drawing on past savings and by greater resort to the unchanged credit facilities. Such borrowing for consumption, other things being assumed equal, will however not be unlimited since borrowers ultimately have to pay attention to their prospective income position. Business is faced with a lower level of demand, and consequent lower profits. In so far as for any particular business demand does decrease, (c) it will not have the same need for credit to maintain an increasing turnover, since working capital and investment requirements will tend to be reduced. (But any rise in costs or compensating opportunities such as might be provided in the export market will work in the opposite direction.) (d) Some temporary borrowing may be needed in the course of adjustment to a lower level of production, e.g. to finance accumulating stocks, but this should be a temporary phenomenon. However (e) undertakings will not all be in the same position; while many may find their need for credit falling, others in expanding sectors may still need increasing amounts of finance to support their natural growth and will have to forgo promising and profitable opportunities and go slow on innovations if they are unable to find it.

Case 2: expanding effective demand checked by tighter fiscal measures, supplemented by tighter credit measures. This is Case 1 plus a credit squeeze: less finance and at a higher cost. The effect of this is to reduce opportunity for consumption to be sustained by borrowing (1 (b) above) and to this extent to lower effective demand still further, so that this could be an appreciable reinforcement in checking consumption expenditure. The need for some temporary finance to deal with accumulating stocks etc. (1 (d)) may raise problems even if it is temporary. Special problems of naturally growing industries (1 (e)) will however be intensified and could lead – if the squeeze is powerful – to the abandonment of developments which otherwise would be thought desirable.

Case 3: expanding effective demand checked by tighter credit measures, fiscal position unchanged. This raises directly the question of how far one could avoid an increase in taxation by tightening up on credit. An unchecked flow of income, continuing to be fed by government expenditure, would have the effect of maintaining the level of consumption. In such circumstances the making of borrowing more difficult would affect the expansion of production more than consumption. As long as income is increasing, consumers are less dependent on borrowing or savings (though the higher standard of living will bring increased commitments by way of hire purchase, for example). But businesses faced with increasing demand are also faced with an accelerating need for extending the scale of their operations; even though current profits increase, restrictions on borrowing could be hitting them hard. With consumption going ahead, a check to production through a fall in the volume of available finance and dearer money could make inflation worse; an easier credit policy might have made possible a larger output to meet the increasing demand. In other words, tight credit alongside an easy fiscal policy could at best be ineffective and at worse could make the position even more inflationary by holding back production more than checking consumption.

To summarise the argument from the three cases considered on our narrow assumptions so far: restrictive fiscal policy by itself can have the effect of controlling demand; restrictive credit policy can reinforce it by discouraging borrowing for consumption purposes; but it could have the effect of restricting the expansion of production more than that of consumption especially when used without being reinforced by fiscal restraint. However, this is a provisional conclusion if taken out of context; before one can put weight on it one must examine the four assumptions with which it has been hedged around.

Before doing this, a short digression should round off the picture. We have been concerned with what happens when effective demand is too high. How would an analysis on similar lines apply to the opposite case of a stagnant economy which required stimulating? The corresponding cases might be called Case 4, stagnant demand stimulated by fiscal concessions alone; Case 5, fiscal concessions plus an easing of credit, and Case 6 an easing of credit unaccompanied by fiscal concessions. The prospects of raising demand would be most favourable in Case 5; indeed in some circumstances it could become too powerful. Case 4 would have some effect provided too restrictive an initial credit policy was not hampering the expansion of production. In Case 6 an easing of credit by itself could well be ineffective, in the absence of reduced taxation or increased government expenditure.

But the stagnant economy as such is not immediately relevant;

stagnation plus rising prices is something different. To revert to
the main thread: analysis of the control of effective demand. The
provisional conclusion – a tighter fiscal policy should restrict consumption generally, but credit restriction could have restrictive
repercussions on production – was based on limiting assumptions
which have to be removed.

These assumptions, it will be recalled, were four: first, that
we were concerned only with a simple problem of preventing
effective demand increasing too fast; second, that fiscal and credit
controls could be made effective without complications; third,
that no account was taken of time lags; and last that other things
could be assumed equal. All these assumptions have important
consequences the nearer one moves to reality.

First, the assumption that all we are concerned with is the
holding back of effective demand. It has already emerged that
there is some inconsistency between restraining consumption on
the one hand and restraining investment on the other. If we look
at policy realistically in circumstances such as those recently
experienced in the U.K., we see a more complex picture. We
were concerned both to hold back current consumption, and to
increase investment with a view to making possible expansion
in the future: first, we are holding back consumption, in order,
second, to switch resources in the direction of investment. Fiscal
action serves to hold back consumption and in the process through
bringing about a general reduction in the profitability of enterprise reduces the volume of investment, although in itself it need
not deter investment by growth enterprises which can in fact see
satisfactory profits ahead. But once we bring in credit restrictions
for the purpose of reinforcing the holding back of consumption,
it has a damaging effect on these growth enterprises as well,
whether through higher rates of interest or through limitations on
the actual volume of credit on offer. How are these enterprises
which it is our intention to continue to encourage to be let out
of the constraint imposed by tighter credit? It should be noted
that this only affects some sectors of enterprise. Much of industry
will be unaffected, since the fall in demand itself has taken off
the pressure for extra finance except possibly in the context
of short-run adjustment. But it is the growth enterprise which we
want to encourage that is in danger of being hard hit.

What then might be done? One is tempted to think of a differential policy: discouragement of loans for consumption purposes, and a higher rate of interest; providing finance freely for approved investment purposes on favourable terms. But the distinction is liable to break down. Expansion is financed out of retained earnings as well as by money raised from outside. The offer of favourable terms by itself for investment purposes would provide an inducement for maximum raising of such concessionary funds, while the money at the company's own disposal through its retained funds could be used in other ways, in the extreme case even being on-lent outside the business. To provide cheaper money alongside dearer money according to the purpose for which it is to be used runs the risk of having to police at least the lender's and possibly all the company's outlays. In general the problem of identification makes it easier to tie up any concession with particular types of transactions which it is desired to encourage rather than relating the concession to particular classifications of borrowed finance.

What this means is that if interest rates are too high or amounts of finance inadequate, direct subsidies in the form of investment grants, for example, may be the appropriate remedy. An alternative would be tax concessions, related to the scale and timing of depreciation. The subsidy has the more direct impact, but may benefit the undeserving; depreciation allowances only benefit those who have been making profits out of which they can recoup themselves if they are to take advantage of the concession, and that may exclude those whom it is most desired to help. But one cannot escape the need for investment incentives, or the problems to which they give rise.

One is impelled to the conclusion that in looking at the working of a restrictive policy one must take into account as part of the same process any measures employed by the government to mitigate the effects of the credit restraint in respect of particular sectors of the economy. The process of imposing restriction and at the same time giving relief cannot be divided. It tailors a general policy to an actual situation. It is not enough to assume that we are concerned only with holding back effective demand. What we want to do is keep consumption demand within bounds while at the same time avoid discouraging new investment in particular ranges of industry, and to do this governments have an armoury of subventions, specialised institutions and tax concessions which must be regarded as part and parcel of the credit policy which they are designed to mitigate.

So much for a closer look at the objective of keeping down effective demand. The next two assumptions to be relaxed can conveniently be taken together. They are that fiscal and credit controls can be taken to the effective, and that time lags in their application are disregarded. One need not doubt that fiscal and credit policy – if applied with sufficient determination – must in time have effects and possibly even devastating effects, but in practice the problem comes down to calculating and ensuring that the effects are such as we wish to see. These calculations must cover many aspects, and among them time lags stand out. None of these effects can show themselves immediately.

In the case of fiscal policy, problems of getting a quick response are well understood. Most changes in taxation take time, for administrative as well as other reasons. This is especially the case in respect of direct taxes. Delay in collecting money is unavoidable. There may be offsetting changes in spending habits. Only the knowledge that it will have to be paid in due course has some effect forthwith.

Indirect taxation can be applied more quickly, in that the effect of an increase in tax on goods can be reflected almost immediately in the price of those goods. The so-called Regulator – the power to increase within limits Purchase Tax and certain excise duties at once without using a budget procedure – is a device to this end which has frequently been used. Similar results to secure quick action, have been ingeniously secured through temporary forced loans. S.E.T. was collected from a wider range of business than ultimately have to pay it, and then refunded after a due interval to those who can show that they are entitled to have their money back. Import Deposits involved money being put up as goods are imported, to be refunded after a given interval. These are both examples of bringing financial pressure forward in time to make the effect of a constraint more immediate; money has to be found now, though to many of the subscribers it will be refunded as of right after a predetermined lapse of time. (To these the cost of finding the money is extra taxation.)

When it comes to credit restriction, rather different considerations apply in respect of efficacy and timing. The main question here concerns the doubt as to how far restrictions on lending can in practice be made effective without leaving loopholes. With hire purchase, the lenders have to be careful to protect their legal position, and therefore to observe regulations, but this did not stop the growth of 'personal' loans. However, if one sets bounds only on the lending of banks, this can be offset by the creation of new institutions, new arrangements and new types of lending outside the banking system proper. With this comes the problem of extending the scope of controls. New sources of lending will no doubt exact a higher price, but at that price the direct impact of the squeeze may be avoided. A squeeze may succeed in preventing those who could usefully expand from doing so; but it cannot be counted on to prevent those who are really determined to get further finance, and who have a certain amount of backing, from getting it at a price, however questionable the purpose. Real estate has attracted to itself a great deal of finance (in part at least at the expense of productive use) which has proved immensely profitable and quite uncontrollable.

There are further complications surounding credit policy. Thus a rise in taxation is reflected in increased demand for credit. In the first instance, before adjustment has taken place, this will take the form of extra borrowing in order to meet the increase in tax liabilities; it is only at a later stage that a lower level of activity should permit a reduction in working capital requirements. Further, the timing varies according to circumstances: existing commitments must largely be followed through until they are finished; prospective commitments can be postponed; but prospective commitments cannot so easily be accelerated in response to an improvement in the economic climate. Lastly, there is an overpowering influence of changing expectations.

This leads to the fourth of the assumptions which we have to remove: that of other things continuing unchanged. However convenient as an analytical device, this is not an assumption which can be maintained since we have to allow for changing expectations (from within) and interruptions (from without). In particular, expected changes in prices have far reaching consequences. If a spender expects prices to rise he will accelerate his purchases; if he expects them to fall, he will hold back. The prospect of rising prices as a result of increased indirect taxation tends in the short term to increase spending. In the long term, faced with the phenomenon of steadily rising prices, spending units – whether private individuals or business enterprises – will adjust their policy in acquiring assets to take account of these developments, whether in the buying of houses and property, or of equities as an alternative to fixed interest securities, or of the new motor car before the price goes up again. The expectation of price increases strengthens the pressure on credit facilities, and in its turn sets other forces in motion. There are repercussions on the relative attractiveness of various types of asset; as expectations change relative prices, the changes in relative prices in their turn work back on the expectations.

Other repercussions to be taken into account are those described as interruptions from without. Policy making – whether fiscal or credit – does not operate in a vacuum. In the real world, the state of the balance of payments, or the prospect of major wage increases, whether starting spontaneously or sparked off by rising prices, are an unavoidable part of the setting.

To summarise the position reached:

(1) Fiscal and credit policy are to a large extent complementary; are not really alternatives; and can at times conflict where the objective is a complicated one, such as restraining consumption while at the same time trying to maintain and increase the expansion of investment.

(2) A tightening of fiscal policy by itself is comprehensive, in that it not only has a direct effect of leaving people with less income to spend and thereby tending to keep down consumption, but indirectly of reducing the prospects and profits and credit requirements of enterprise.

(3) A tightening of credit policy supplements fiscal policy in so far as it discourages borrowing for consumption as a way round the fiscal constraints; this may be important if there is an expectation of rising prices continuing.

(4) A tightening of credit policy unaccompanied by any tightening on the fiscal side is unlikely to hold back consumption, but by holding back investment could in theory make inflation worse by its adverse effects on production; in practice it may merely

prove ineffective, but one can envisage it becoming a serious obstacle to increasing output.

(5) Fiscal and credit measures cannot be treated in isolation, and account must be taken of:

    (a) Subsidies or special financial arrangements introduced to alleviate the pressure of less and dearer finance on any particular industries which it is desirable to stimulate.

    (b) Careful assessment of the effects of a given piece of restriction on other parts of the economy.

    (c) Measures to determine the timing, given the existence of time lags.

    (d) Proper allowance for consequential reactions to the measures both within the economy (e.g. in respect of prices or wages) and outside it as a result of their impact elsewhere.

The implications of all this are significant.

It stands out that one cannot be content with general conclusions about credit restrictions. Restriction is and must be accompanied by concessions and facilities safeguarding the sensitive sections of the economy. Not only has one to identify what these may be, but one then has to go on to assess at the same time the impact of both restrictions and concessions. At all times we have to bear in mind both the particular and the general.

This is a conclusion of substance. In the case of fiscal policy the particular methods chosen to increase revenue are chosen with care, among other reasons because the way in which the money is raised will affect the balance between consumption and saving. It is not so generally recognised that the disturbance in continuity arising from a sharp tightening of credit facilities – whether in volume or in cost – has uneven effects. The reduction of effective demand by itself will affect different sectors of an expanding economy in different ways, since rates of expansion vary. Some sectors will be marking time and ceasing to expand as demand falls; others will need to expand only slowly; others again, in spite of the general fall in demand, will find themselves faced with a continuing increase in business. There is nothing to stop them continuing to expand, or to switch to cheaper goods if that is appropriate, as long as credit facilities are not cut back. But once credit facilities do become more difficult, these are the ones for which the restraint is most significant. If the object of policy is to slow down consumption while maintaining production, discrimination is necessary, since a general cut back in credit must militate against those sectors most in need of it. Such discrimination takes the form of compensating or exempting the particular sectors involved from the pressure exerted so powerfully upon them. Easier terms for exports, subsidies or tax concessions for new investment, special support for industries in development areas, are an integral part of an effective credit policy. The constraints and reliefs go together.

3. *Impact on the Individual Enterprise*

The dicussion so far has been in overall terms. One needs to see the position from the standpoint of the individual producer, say a manufacturer.

A manufacturing company will find its room for manoeuvre circumscribed by its receipts, its payments and its finance to bridge the gap, something as follows:

1. *Receipts*
   Sales: the proceeds coming in after an interval

2. *Payments*
   (i) *Wages* (and salaries): must be paid regularly
   (ii) *Interest and short-term market borrowings:* fixed amounts on due dates
   (iii) *Materials and components:* perhaps some elasticity in payments
   (iv) *Rent, rates and taxes:* fairly promptly
   (v) *Maintenance and replacement:* some postponement – at a cost
   (vi) *Remuneration of proprietors:* dividends etc., out of profits
   (vii) *Additions to plant and equipment*

3. *Finance*
   (i) *Permanent capital and past accumulations*

   (ii) *Fixed term loans:* renewable at intervals
   (iii) *Bank facilities*, revolving within a set limit
   (iv) *Other short term facilities:* probably based on anticipating earnings or postponing outgoings

Within such a framework the manufacturer is faced with making ends meet.

To begin with – let us assume – the business is turning over satisfactorily. Receipts from sales are coming in after the usual interval on a scale sufficient to cover payments, given that the business already has basic finance at its disposal and access to bank or other supporting finance adequate for its needs.

Now the position changes, in what seems to the manufacturer to be a very satisfactory direction: his sales go up substantially and look like staying up, and the price is right. The following things happen:

(a) The goods have to go out before the money comes in.
(b) More money has to be found for wages because more hours have to be worked. (We assume wage rates unchanged.) Wage payments cannot be delayed.
(c) Increased purchases of materials and components. These have to be paid for in a reasonable time; delay may mean higher prices (discounts forgone) and in due course a limitation on supplies.
(d) If sales continue to increase and the market to expand, sooner or later more money will be needed for additions to plant and equipment to enlarge capacity.

In the absence of financial stringency, these problems are solved without difficulty. The banks increase their loans until the amount outstanding reaches a level where a market issue is appropriate. A merchant bank takes over and finds any extra finance needed until the issue can be underwritten and subscribed. The capital market is there to perform its normal function. After all, we are assuming a profitable business faced with an expanding market.

What happens, however, in squeeze conditions when the bank is not prepared to contemplate a sufficient increase in its lending, and the prospects in the capital market are unfavourable? No one will want to make an issue of Ordinary shares at a knock-down price, or borrow for a long time ahead at high rates of interest which are liable to fall once inflation ends. In any case, it may be impossible to get the money because of the crowd of would-be borrowers. Room for manoeuvre is limited. Wages must be paid. Money due from customers might be accelerated, and that due to suppliers delayed, but there is a clash of interest both ways and it will not be easy to alter the balance between creditors and debtors very far. Some tax payments may be delayed at a price. There might be some postponement on maintenance and replacement, but this can only be temporary if it is not to do damage. One can avoid increasing dividends, perhaps, even if the profits could justify an increase, but one cannot cut the dividend without weakening the credit of the company.

The list of items due for payment set out above follows an approximate hierarchical order reflecting the difficulty of avoiding or delaying payment. The item 'additions to plant and equipment' is at the bottom of the list, but heads the candidates for cutting. Expansion – profitable expansion – is out if it involves a major outlay on new investment. What is more, potential customers may have to be dropped anyway, if the bank is not prepared to finance a larger wage bill and more expenditure on supplies. All that is left for the company to do is to search around for some supplementary source of finance which may enable it to salvage some of the prospective business.

One must stress again that this economic allegory is based on the most generous assumptions about the profitability of the business and the excellence of the prospects; this does not save us from a melancholy conclusion. The moral remains: prolonged pressure on credit – unless it is alleviated by incentives and inducements – must militate against investment and expansion, even if the prospects and profits are good.

Our allegory can be made to yield further illuminating results. In particular, it can help to answer three related questions. The first is: what happens to the company if there is a fall in demand, instead of a rise? The second is: what happens if the company is faced with a large wages claim? The third is: what happens if the company goes ahead and expands output, evading its bank manager until it has taken on the new business relying on its profitability?

A fall in demand – once it has made itself felt – will ultimately be translated into less time worked and less materials used. The flow of materials and bought-in components wll be lower than before, and there will be a reduction in the wages bill. The flow of receipts for goods sold on credit will continue for the time being at the old (higher) level, and will come down gradually to the new (lower) level over an interval. In the earlier stages there may be an accumulation of unsold stocks, but as this is worked off the need for working capital diminishes as long as the business continues to cover its costs. (But some could find this a slow process.) The upshot is that there is less need for bank finance because of the fall in demand. Generalise this sequence of cause and effect, and the conclusion is that a cut in demand resulting from fiscal action carries with it some fall in the amount of credit required.

This assumes a company which is continuing to cover its costs. If the company were hit so hard that it continued to be unable to cover costs and had no prospect of doing so, sooner or later it would be out of business. But it is conceivable that in the earlier phases of its decline it would have a superfluity of cash coming in as the outcome of earlier sales, while the outgoings fell off drastically because the output would not find buyers. (While this is a legitimate theoretical example, one must concede at once that many companies facing misfortune are likely to be short of cash).

This brings in a vital distinction. The doomed company may have an easy cash position; the prosperous company (discussed just before) may have very serious problems of liquidity and be turning away prospective customers. This is a point which will be taken further later, but in the meantime one notes that it is the prosperous and expanding company which is inhibited by anti-inflationary credit constraints from adding to the supply of goods which would mitigate inflation.

The second question related to the company faced with a large wage claim. The simple answer is that if it can it will raise prices. But if it has not got this room for manoeuvre – for example, because it would lose too much business if it raised prices – it would be forced to turn to the possibility of reducing its outlay. It might be able to do something by way of increased productivity: that is, maintain output while employing fewer people (at a larger cost per head) or by making other economies, but once such possibilities are exhausted, the residual item in the list is the sufferer. Expansion – in the form of additions to plant and equipment – and the profits that go with expansion, will have to be forgone, together with any increase in productivity that might have come from operating on a larger scale. The wage bill and expansion are competing alternatives, and at the crunch the wage bill wins.

The third question relates to the prosperous company with attractive prospects before it, but short on the financial side. What happens if it ignores its lack of liquidity, and goes ahead hoping that the demonstrable excellence and profitability of its business will see it through? The logical answer is that it could discover that it had not enough money to pay the wage bill on the Friday.

This might mean that the company went out of business altogether, but on the assumption that it is a highly successful business it is likely that with the help of its reluctant bank manager it will secure a fresh injection of capital on conditions. The business may continue, but the price of the rescue money may be very exacting indeed. The newcomers will expect an appropriately high share of the profits and will want to take over control in order to protect themselves, and at the end of it the original proprietors could find that they have lost the business and are working for strangers.

This case of the successful business caught through over-trading provides the basis for an important general proposition. One must draw a distinction between undertakings in difficulty because they cannot carry on at a profit – the case envisaged in simple theory – and the very different category of expanding undertakings threatened with being brought to a sudden stop because they have failed to assure themselves of the finance necessary to reach the scale necessary to maximise their profits. If we describe the latter process as financial embarrassment and the former as financial failure, the fact is that financial stringency may cause embarrassment to prosperous companies at a much earlier stage than it brings failure to companies unable to earn a profit. But even before this point is reached, hand to hand working could lead to delay, with higher costs and lengthening delivery dates, bringing with it lower profits and fewer future orders, and these on less favourable terms.

People have to plan the scale of their operations in the light of the finance available to them. If with a good business they are too ambitious, they may lose their business or a large part of it, but it could continue with the profits going to others. If a business is a failure and cannot earn a profit, it will cease to exist or its resources will be diverted to some quite different form of activity.

The point of this argument is that financial pressure affects and constricts economically justifiable activities; it is not a matter – as some might be inclined to suppose – of financial stringency revealing bad businesses for what they are and driving them into deserved bankruptcy. The expansion of the deserving may be the first to feel the pressure.

We arrive, from the angle of the individual firm, at the same conclusion as that of the preceding section, that there is a delicate balance to be maintained, and that constraints and reliefs go together. And this must be supplemented with a further conclusion: that if business is kept short of finance for fear that it will be used to enter into inflationary wage settlements, the same shortage is likely to restrict even more sharply the increase of productive investment.

Indeed, one can press the argument very much further. It is probable that there will be some cases where a business kept short of funds would be more likely to accede to inflationary wage demands in an inflationary situation. On the one hand, it will have the choice of agreeing to the wage demands, with good prospects of being able to pass on the costs in the form of higher prices. On the other, it has the alternative of facing a strike with adverse effects on cash flow which, with constraints on borrowing and existing commitments to nvestment expenditure, could precipitate an acute liquidity crisis. The attractions of the former course should not be underrated.

4. *Investment Incentives*

When fiscal and credit pressure is being applied to hold back the level of consumption, the problem of protecting and encouraging productive investment becomes an urgent one. To deal with inflation we need to control demand and to stimulate supply, and it is not easy to do both at the same time. British governments, whatever their political complexion, have always recognised the need for such action whether by means of subsidies or tax concessions or facilities directed to particular developments. The policy objective is accepted.

The point now to be discussed may appear somewhat narrow, but it raises matters of principle and practice. It is concerned with the question: should the encouragement of investment basically be profit-oriented or prospect-oriented? The question itself requires explanation.

In essence this is the argument between investment grants and investment allowances. The Labour Government favoured the method of grants in respect of any investment project which fell within the framework of the rules of the scheme which was being operated. The Conservative Government has reverted to a system of allowances, giving tax relief in respect of outlay on investment. The main argument for the change is that 'investment grants benefit firms whether or not they are making profit and they can therefore result in an uneconomic investment leading to waste of resources'.* Subsidiary arguments are that the then existing scheme discriminated unjustifiably against the service industries, and that it involved a (presumably avoidable) administrative burden on both industry and government. One must take it that it was the first argument which proved conclusive in leading the Conservative Government 'to decide to replace investment grants with tax allowances and reductions to help promote the conditions likely to stimulate higher investment'.

The effect of the new policy – hence the use of the term 'profit-oriented' – is that expansion is encouraged because undertakings that invest their profits in expanding their business are relieved

* *Investment Incentives* (Cmnd. 4516 of October 1970). In March 1972 substantial extensions were announced, taking the form of improved tax allowances for investment, and regional development grants in cash. See *Industrial and Regional Development* (Cmnd. 4942 of March 1972).

of taxation. It has the practical consequence that the businesss must be earning enough profits to get the benefit of the concession. This provides, or so it could be argued, an automatic test of success and competence, and if 'to him that hath shall be given' seems to some a crude yardstick for so complicated a matter, it clearly is administratively convenient. The policy has built into it a bias in favour of encouraging firms in proportion to their success, but by implication leaves the less successful in the cold. Indeed the official argument goes further by implying that the alternative policy is more likely to result in uneconomic investment leading to waste of resources.

It is here that doubts appear. Assuming that the financial benefit to a firm is the same either way, it is a matter of indifference whether it takes the form of tax concession or of a positive payment. But by definition, the less successful firm loses, if it has not got the profits against which to charge the depreciation. And it is at this point that the doubts begin to be strengthened. It can be argued that the less successful firm in any case starts with an initial handicap: it has to find its share of the money for the expansion, for the grant only covers a proportion of the cost. It must therefore have above-average prospects if it is to secure the necessary additional finance. Of course, what happens can lead to uneconomic investment and waste of resources – but this will have to be paid for by somebody who has been persuaded to commit himself to back the expansion. To believe otherwise is to believe that only the successful are worth encouraging, and that encouragement should be withheld from those who are not so successful even if they can find others who are prepared to back a new development. This may be sensible doctrine if expansion overall is proceeding too fast, but not otherwise.

But to be relevant the analysis must put the question into its context. The question applies to a specific set of circumstances: conditions of stringency imposed in order to control demand, but at the same time a need for encouraging expansion of supply. The question itself is concerned with alternatives of profit-oriented or prospect-oriented investment: investment encouraged by tax concessions on profits earned, as opposed to providing supplementary finance for investment which can command the necessary minimum of new money on the strength of the prospects it offers. What are the characteristics we should look for in the investment to be encouraged?

It is submitted that there are three in particular:* that the demand for the output should be income-elastic; that production should be capital intensive; and that it should offer prospects of profitable continuity under competitive conditions in the long term. By the first is meant that the added output should be of a kind likely to encounter a demand rising at an above average rate as the income of the community increases. (The converse of this is that when the income of the community is being kept down, the restriction will bear rather more heavily than average on the output in question; with the implication that its current profitability is unlikely to be high.) The second requirement is that it should be capital intensive: that the expansion should take the form of modernisation and mechanisation rather than of increased demand for labour; we are here talking about encouraging investment on its own merits, and are not concerned with the rather different problem of employment-giving developments in depressed areas. The last requirement is that the proposed expansion should offer a future in terms of steady development under conditions when prices were no longer subject to continuous rises, but finance was available for good business freely and on more normal terms.

These conditions are relevant both to the case of profit-oriented enterprises earning enough to enable them to take full advantage of concessions in respect of investment allowances, and to that of less fortunate enterprises which are not in such a strong position for reasons which may be beyond their control. But in the case of the latter prospect-oriented enterprises we come up against this difficulty. One can agree that just to confine the benefits to the profit-earners may not be enough; one can accept that if a business has such good prospects that it can attract the necessary finance from outside to enable it to expand with the help offered by government, it should have the opportunity. But what do we mean by attracting finance from outside? A genuine injection of outside finance put up by responsible investors can be a cogent

---

* These tests, which look to longer term prospects, are not relevant in certain classes of cases – e.g. developments giving immediate and needed employment, or which remove economic bottlenecks – where clearly quite different conditions may apply.

argument for the government going in also. But this is not an automatic guarantee that responsible judgement has been passed on the proposed development. A badly managed company can drift into the position where an ill-considered investment project is started on the strength of its limited assets and carried to completion with government money; when it is completed the company may have run itself short of working capital, maybe accepting orders which in practice are likely to bring losses rather than profits in order to keep going, and in other ways may be heading for disaster. In short, there are strong arguments for supporting prospect-oriented enterprises when it is in the public interest to stimulate investment and growth, but it cannot be an undiscriminating support.

To sum up, when investment expansion needs to be encouraged one cannot depend on tax concessions alone. But there is no automatic method of supporting undertakings with good long-term prospects which have been held back by imposed cuts in demand or by shortage of funds. There is a considerable area of decision-making to be handled, which calls for administrative, institutional and managerial effort to determine who are the deserving and how they are best helped.

5. The Book-keeping of Inflation: Asset Valuations and Rates of Return

The problem so far has been one of holding back demand, while at the same time maintaining and encouraging investment; if prices are to be kept from rising, we need both a restrained demand and an increased output to meet it. The next stage is to examine the effects of rising prices.

Changing price levels create a discrepancy between money values attributed to items in balance sheets and their underlying real values. With rising prices valuations put on properties or other assets acquired in the past, and in the books at original cost, understate the real value to an extent which increases as prices go up. Other items also tend to trail behind current values.

This effect is most noticeable in the case of real estate. The knowledge that prices are likely to go on rising makes the purchase of such property all the more attractive, and prices escalate, so that the modest figure at which freehold properties stand in balance sheets usually bears little relationship to the market prices realised for similar properties when they are bought and sold.

Rising prices have distorting effects in other ways also. Thus in respect of money borrowed at fixed interest on long term, rising prices impose loss on those whom the money is owed: on the one hand, the purchasing power of their fixed income is falling; or the other, the market value of their security will also have fallen in so far as interest rates have risen since the debt was created. Their loss is the gain of the proprietors of the business, who hold the equity. This is because the money value of the physical assets tends to increase, while the fixed sum the company has to pay anually represents less and less in terms of purchasing power. Furthermore the business is likely to be paying on the basis of a rate of interest agreed at a time when rates were lower. This comes home to the proprietors of a business only when the loan matures and has to be repaid; when that happens if it is to be replaced it will be at the higher current rate of interest, and so will take a larger share of the profits.

The outcome of this is to make profits look higher in money terms than they actually are. Working on the conventional basis of historic cost, money set aside for depreciation only amortises the (lower) price at which a physical asset was originally acquired. When it has to be replaced, more will have to be found to pay the higher cost, unless special provision has been made. With an inadequate cash flow extra money will have to be brought in from outside, again at a rate of interest which is likely to be higher. Costs would have been understated to the extent that special provisions for replacement at higher values has not been made. The corollary of this is that profits will have been overstated.

The same phenomenon is present in the case of working capital. A business needs funds to pay the wage bill, and to maintain its working stock of materials and components. The cost of all these is rising. If one sells off items from output at what they cost to produce, new money will have to be injected to finance the increase in future costs. Only if such products are sold at a price sufficient to cover the cost of replacing them, can the undertaking be said to cover its full cost. (Hence the danger of fixed price contracts if they take time to complete.)

The habit of looking to past costs as opposed to current (replacement) costs is reinforced in two ways. In the first place, there is an unwillingness to raise prices to the full extent, partly from an inherent distaste of doing so except under circumstances of demonstrable necessity, and partly because of the fear that competitors will not follow suit but may maintain lower prices in an attempt to win a larger share of the trade. But a second reason is perhaps more important. The tax system operates on realised money profits, and not profits after subtracting the higher replacement costs. The addition to cost required to keep capital intact in real terms is not allowed as a charge against tax liability.

Under conventional accounting methods a company will therefore have to acquire new finance to meet price rises even though in physical terms the business is unchanged. Where then has the money gone to? The beneficiaries are the customers, the revenue and possibly also the equity shareholders. If costs had been calculated on a replacement basis, the customers would have had to pay more. If the tax collector was not compelled to make his assessment on the basis of past costs, he would have received less because the replacement cost would have been higher. Equity shareholders may be gainers in so far as fixed interest lenders (who originally provided finance when purchasing power was higher and interest rates lower) are the losers, but their gain will depend on dividend policy. One should not regard ordinary shareholders as permanent beneficiaries as they may have a day of reckoning to come; in particular, if assets are not properly replaced, it is the equity holders who suffer.

Companies are of course aware of these consequences of conventional book-keeping in an inflationary situation, and make some attempt to take account of it. A few companies seek to make real valuations in respect of their position, or show the effect of introducing replacement costing. Others make special provision (in spite of the tax which has to be paid in the course of doing so). Most companies probably try to make some provision if they can, but in many cases much outside money is already needed to finance a given level of activity, let alone an increased level in real terms.

New outside money is of course likely to be expensive, compared with outside money brought in at some time in the less
immediate past. Industrial debentures towards the end of 1971
had to provide something like 10 per cent. For companies making
profits, this is alleviated by the extent to which they save tax.
(The payment is made out of profits before tax). There is no such
alleviation as long as a company is not making profits.

At this point one must pause to look at the position of the new
debenture holders who are subscribing currently on the basis of
receiving 10 per cent. The sum is of course reduced in most cases
by income tax, and the holders are aware that their 10 per cent
may still be eroded by continuing inflation. But one cannot
assume that rapidly rising prices will continue indefinitely when
increasing efforts are being made to check the rise. And here we
come to a climax. What happens if rising prices are brought to a
halt? (It is not quite beyond the bounds of possibility that when
the turning point comes there might even be some reduction in
prices before they started levelling off.)

To begin with the beneficiaries. The biggest loser previously
was the lender of some time back on fixed interest. He will have
seen the purchasing power of his fixed income fall and his rate of
interest remaining far below the level at which later current investments were taking place. He now gains some compensation to the
extent that the continuing loss of purchasing power has ceased,
and interest rates may fall, thereby increasing the capital value of
his security. In contrast, his successor – the lender at 10 per cent –
becomes a real beneficiary. Not only does his 10 per cent (heavily
loaded to anticipate future price rises) become stable in terms of
purchasing power, but possibly even increases a little. The market
rate of interest will start tumbling below 10 per cent as soon as
the stabilising of the price situation makes it clear that such a
rate is too good to continue. He will have his firm contract and
his stable money. He gains where his predecessor lost; his successor will have to be content with less. He himself is the conspicuous
beneficiary; he took the risk that prices might go on rising, but
they have stabilised – and this is his reward.

The company which borrowed from him at 10 per cent is in a
less happy position. It has to go on paying 10 per cent come what
may, until the period of the loan expires. 10 per cent, no longer

reinforced by rising prices, becomes a burden which eats into what is left of profits for equity holders. Worse still, if profits cease, there will be no tax available against which to charge an appropriate portion of the 10 per cent. Instead of prices being kept too low because no account is to be taken of replacement cost, they will tend to be kept up to cover past obligations, at a time when demand (in money terms) is showing little or no increase. The pressure on business loaded with a heavy weight of debt contracted on onerous terms through the need to keep pace with rising prices could become intense. To keep on earning 10 per cent in an economy where competition is keeping prices relatively stable and proceeds are not being topped up by inflation may become unmanageable, even though the need to find extra finance to meet rising costs has been removed.

The long term rate of interest is affected by expectations. Is 10 per cent for industrial debentures a high rate or not? Historically it is a high rate. From the point of view of a lender it just about makes it worth his while to lend, given that he has to pay tax and that out of his taxed income he expects to have to make provision for a decreasing purchasing power of money. From the point of view of the borrower, it is not so onerous if he pays the interest out of untaxed profits and expects to repay the principal with money which is losing purchasing power. But this is on the expectation of rising prices. The moment prices cease to rise (and far more if they begin to fall) the positions are reversed. 10 per cent becomes a very handsome return in stable money terms, and the borrower discovers he has contracted a very burdensome obligation.

In settled economic conditions contracts embodying long-term obligations start from the assumption of certain stabilities, and in particular an element of stability both in prices and long-term rates of interest. On this basis long-term interest rates remain sticky: borrowing on long term usually means funding, and when one funds one does not agree to pay slightly more for long-term money if one can get the going rate by waiting. One just keeps one's place in the queue until a favourable opportunity occurs, continuing with short-term debts until one's turn comes. In such conditions long-term rates are stable, and people wait their turn borrowing in other ways in the meanwhile.

But none of this holds good in unsettled times when price levels are on the move and the value of money is changing. In such circumstances long-term fixed interest finance becomes unattractive because of the uncertainty, and less suitable for business. Equity finance is more adaptable and adjusts itself to changes, although there may be tax complications. Shorter term borrowing may be preferred to longer term. New types of security carrying provisions for adjustment are developed: for example convertibles on fixed rates but with an option to exchange into equities, or even in some cases loans with a provision for changing the rate at intervals in the light of current interest movements. Such arrangements help to preserve a fair division of risk and advantage between borrower and lender. The concept of a stable long-term rate of interest loses meaning when investors are choosing where to place their money on the basis of expectations of capital gains as much as of fixed and certain incomes in money terms. But the general effect of disturbed conditions will tend to be a greater volume of short-term borrowings, and a considerably lower level of activity in the long-term stock markets.

The real source of disturbance is to be found in changes of expectations, rather than in the expectations themselves. The trouble begins when expectations are changed by events. If, after a continuing rise over a period of years, prices suddenly settle down and the price level is stabilised, debt burdens contracted under the influence of inflation may prove unmanageable, and commitments entered into in quite different conditions are shown to have been made on mistaken assumptions. In the 1950's UK local authorities borrowed on short-term because they expected long-term rates to come down, and the volume of short-term local governmental debt has been at spectacular levels ever since. Long-term rates have risen steadily, and the local authorities are still waiting for a favourable opportunity to fund. Another example is that of the Agricultural Mortgage Corporation between the wars. When interest rates fell farmers who had borrowed at high rates wanted to repay and reborrow at lower rates. The Corporation on the other hand was in trouble because it had raised a large part of its money on fixed interest terms while the rates were still high.

The situation which would be created by falling interest rates is complicated by the diversity of the positions of the borrowers involved. Some borrowers will have succeeded in making arrangements which put them into a position to repay and so get the benefit of the lower rates. Others will have been forced to commit themselves, and they in their turn can find their capital structure undermined. For policy makers this is a difficult situation with which to deal, since arrangements to meet one set of problems could give unconvenanted benefits to those who had succeeded in avoiding these particular difficulties, while failing to help others with different problems. A major change in rates can have damaging consequences, but different people will be affected in different ways: quite simply, some gain, some lose.

Up to this point the relationship between borrower and lender has been treated from the standpoint of finance for business. But the largest borrower is the government, normally (though not necessarily) a substantial net borrower when the needs of local authorities and public industries are taken into account; this of course is not just current expenditure, but includes a large amount of investment. The existence of such borrowing influences rates of interest and this in its turn has repercussions on the terms which industry can get for its finance.

Official borrowing can take a number of forms: long-term loans at one end of the scale and Treasury bills and equally short borrowing by local authorities, as well as borrowing from the banks, at the other. The motives prompting the public authorities in their choice of the form of borrowing are mixed and contradictory. The first motive which suggests itself is that of keeping the interest due to be paid as low as possible, but (assuming that the actual borrowing operations are administered efficiently) borrowing cheaply for its own sake cannot be a dominant consideration as far as the government is concerned. The management of a public debt has to be so conducted as to take account of its substantial influence on interest rates – in particular relative interest rates – since what the authorities do will have repercussions on the cost and supply of finance to business and the movement of funds across the exchanges. How the government manages its debts – although it would be a mistake to regard its capacity to do so as unqualified, given the exposed position of sterling as an international currency – will have a wide range of repercussions on the future development of the economy. Taking the longer view, this means above all taking into consideration the desirability of speeding up or slowing down the pace of the economy, with its consequential effects on output, employment and price movements. If the government finds itself with an opportunity for borrowing cheaply, it will be because the economy needs stimulating and cheaper money is desirable on general grounds, as in 1932 onwards. The forcing down of interest rates in funding the debt after the last war was an unhappy exception.

Such considerations affect not only the level of interest rates generally, but the form in which the authorities seek to borrow. Short-term borrowing may appear cheap and easy, but it leaves the holders of these short-term assets with an opportunity to turn them into cash (and through cash into goods) should they suddenly come to expect prices to move upwards. And short-term borrowing may in its turn provide the foundation for an expansion of bank credit when such an expansion is not thought desirable. On the other hand borrowing on long-term leaves the public with assets which they cannot dispose of at their original value if there is a general movement to turn them into more liquid assets, since long-term rates of interest would rise and the capital value of the securities go down. Prospective purchasers of such securities will limit the amount of money they are prepared to put up for the purchase of long-term securities at going rates, and the volume passing through the markets will be less. Nor can it be assumed that if the rate is sharply raised (to encourage buyers) then the public will increase its purchases of government securities; it could indeed become alarmed at the prospect of still further rises in rates and increase its reluctance to take up government securities. There is a delicate balance to be observed between keeping the long-term rate relatively stable, and risking in the process not offering enough to the investing public to persuade it to go on investing, and letting interest rates rise too far or too fast, so that the resulting fall in capital values frightens the public out of investing in gilt-edged. The management of the debt is especially difficult as long as the public authorities are on balance substantial net borrowers. In the opposite case, by cutting investment and other expenditure and raising taxes, the government may put itself into a much stronger position as far as debt management taken by itself is concerned, but deflationary or other uncomfortable consequences may present it with difficulties of the opposite kind.

Conditions of instability – and of price instability in particular – therefore present the authorities with problems not unlike those faced by private industry but without the possibility of borrowing on equities. If prices are going up, this will find reflection in long-term interest rates that go up if long-term borrowing is to continue on any scale. If prices are going down and expected to continue going down, interest rates will have to come down also. The instability will be reflected not only in short-term rates, which are expected to move more freely and where borrowers and lenders are only committed for short periods, but also in long-term rates, which are dominated by the assumption that expectations remain unchanged.

One consequence of this will be that at a turning point, such as when inflation is expected to cease, one must be prepared to see a great increase in the need for short-term borrowing both on private account and on government account. The crucial point here is whether inflation is in fact coming to an end. If price rises do cease, no one will have an inducement to increase the rate of his purchases merely because he finds it easier to borrow from his bank. On the other hand if price rises continue, people will be in a position to make a profit from purchases financed by banks. But to hold back financial facilities when there is an expectation that prices are ceasing to rise makes for worse trouble since producers output may be checked. Since the alternative for producers is borrowing on longer term, and long-term rates are as high as they are only because regular price rises are built into them, no one will borrow in that way till the long-term rates have in fact fallen.

What this comes to is that with an expected turning point a consistent decision is required. Once it has been decided to increase spending power (the fiscal concession) it is folly to hold back on borrowing facilities for business. With long-term rates abnormally high, business will not be able to enter prudently into long-term commitments on a 10 per cent basis, while lenders will hesitate to accept less. That is where the need for sufficient short-term finance comes in. At a later stage, with the credit squeeze relaxed and long-term rates down in response to increasing confidence that the rise in prices is moderating or ceasing, there will be opportunities for funding and raising money on the stock market to pay off the outstanding short-term commitments. But to hold back on financial facilities while increasing spending power is to hold back the growth of output and endanger the strategy. Further, the expansion of output requires the accumulation of stocks of materials and components in advance of production. There must be an expansion of working capital to be financed by an expansion of credit, as well as some deterioration in the current balance of payments on account of imported materials and components. Some increase in bank lending and some deterioration in the balance of payments must be accepted if one is to get past the crucial turning point.

But we are not yet out of the wood. Not all business undertakings will be in a position to borrow even short-term finance at favourable rates, let alone long-term finance on impossible terms. In many cases balance sheets are likely to have been seriously distorted by the previous inflationary period. How can they be reinforced?

In some cases business concerns will have substantial fixed assets shown at an unduly low figure in their accounts. Could these be written up? The writing up of assets is a reasonable operation after values have reached some stability. It is more dubious at the outset, while the period of uncertainty persists. Of course there is much to be said in theory in favour of a realistic rate of return being shown on capital employed. But one cannot assume that such a change in such circumstances would improve the borrowing power of the undertaking, since on the reassessment the return of the amount of capital employed (now increased, with the rate of return correspondingly reduced) may not impress the prospective investors. Against this, companies which have valuable collateral assets should be able to improve their borrowing power if such assets appear at a proper figure. However, the reassessment of balance sheet figures after a period of inflation is a matter for the accounting profession, who are uncomfortably aware of it.

The normal approach would look to a reduction in company taxation as the appropriate method of reinforcing the capital position, but waiting for retained profits to build up could prove too slow. One may need other methods of government action to reinforce the liquidity position of industry as quickly as possible if we are to get early increases in output. Special measures could become imperative, since – as it were – we have to round the corner without skidding into the wall.

It should perhaps be made clear that this is being written on the basis of a fairly specific hypothesis. It is meaningful in a situation where the pressure of events – rising prices and rising unemployment – has led to some sort of a concordat between labour and industry, designed to secure a workable incomes and prices policy. There is agreement that early expansion is essential. The resources for this are unused and available. Money demand will be there on an adequate scale. What the present argument is addressed to is the danger that the financial position of business has been so eroded that it is not in a position to expand.

What action could the government take? The lending power of the banks could (and would) be increased. Some move back towards investment grants? Some reincarnation of I.R.C.? A combination of the two, to make investment grants more selective? One possibility might be the quick injection of finance, if circumstances made it necessary, in the form of interest-free government loans (interest-free at any rate for an initial period) accompanied perhaps by terms which encouraged early repayment out of profits (though this will involve agreement with the banks as to where their lending stands). However, these are not issues to be pursued at this point. The present purpose of this argument is to establish the existence of a possible danger, leaving the question of how it might be dealt with for later.

6. Wage Determination and Consumer Prices

Preoccupation with the financial mechanism must not blind us to a situation which goes far wider: one of rising prices and rising unemployment, both threatening to increase, during a continuous period of fiscal and credit squeeze of unprecedented severity which was only being relaxed in 1971. Above all, what are we to make of the arrival on this scene of what we have come to call a wages explosion?

There are further features which are hard to explain. Rising prices (and unemployment) are not domestic matters confined to the U.K. but are spread throughout the world. The inflationary tendency should be associated – one would expect – with a boom in construction, coming from the flow of money going into bricks and mortar, on the assumption that with rising prices and costs any building is likely to increase in value. Leaving aside developments in big office blocks, the U.K. building industry has been somewhat depressed. Strangest of all is the association of rising wages and prices with rising unemployment, and not over-employment.

The dimensions of the problem are conveniently illustrated by the movement of earnings in manufacturing and of retail prices.

Manufacturing Earnings and Retail Prices: U.K. 1965–71
(Increase on Previous Year %)

	Earnings	Prices	Excess of Earnings
1965	6·9	4·8	2·1
1966	6·1	3·9	2·2
1967	3·3	2·5	0·8
1968	8·5	4·7	3·8
1969	8·0	5·4	2·6
1970	12·6	6·4	6·2
1971	11·3	9·4	1·9

(Source: *Monthly Digest of Statistics*)

One has to explain two distinct aspects: on the one hand, the general upward pressure of wages, and on the other increased escalation especially after the middle of 1969. It should also be noted that the percentage of registered unemployment, which had stood at 2·2 per cent in July 1969 and at 2·5 per cent in July 1970, was up to 3·5 per cent in July 1971, and over 4 per cent by the end of the year.

First, the general upward wage pressure. This has continued since the end of the war, and in the ten years up to 1966 the compound rate of increase works out at a little over 4 per cent per annum for weekly wage rates in the U.K. (The big jump came later.) This continuing rise can be most carefully examined in the context of the relationship between productivity and wage changes. It has been observed that if the benefits of productivity increases are taken up in the form of increased remuneration for those most closely concerned with it, there is nothing left for others whose occupation is not such as to give scope for productivity increases. But the implications of this have now been the subject of a comprehensive analysis* by H. A. Turner and D. A. S. Jackson who appear to have established that there is a world-wide pattern. Summarised, their conclusions are these:

(1) The pace is set by average money wages rising at the same rate as productivity per head in those industrial branches where productivity naturally tends to rise fastest.

(2) Average *real* wages tend to rise at a pace equal to average productivity growth. By definition they cannot rise beyond it.

(3) Retail prices tend to rise at a rate roughly corresponding to the difference between money wage increases and average productivity growth – i.e. the rise bridges the gap.

To illustrate: if a normal inter-industry rate of growth is from 0 to 7 per cent annually and money wages increase at approaching 7 per cent a year, prices will tend to rise $3\frac{1}{2}$ per cent annually on average, and real wages will also rise by $3\frac{1}{2}$ per cent.

These conclusions are arrived at after examining changes in wages and consumer prices from 1956–65 in advanced 'market' economies, in 'planned' economies (but not including the U.S.S.R. and China) and in less developed economies. Over 50 countries are covered. In the case of 19 advanced 'market' economies the increase per annum from 1956 to 1965 (mean of country averages) was 6·4 per cent in money wages, 3·0 per cent in prices, 3·3 per cent in real wages. For 32 less developed economies the corresponding figures were 6·6 per cent, 3·4 per cent and 3·3 per cent. (This selection excludes the Argentine, Brazil and Chile, where inflationary pressures were exceptional.) The figures for four 'planned' economies were 4·4 per cent, 0·6 per cent and 3·8 per cent. (Bulgaria, East Germany, Hungary, Poland, with Yugoslavia deliberately excluded.)

The pattern is world wide. This resulting 'wage leadership/ cost inflation model for the world as a whole' reflects three recognisable forms of business behaviour: where productivity is rising,

* 'On the Determination of the General Wage Level – a World Analysis', *Economic Journal*, December 1970.

firms prefer to concede wage increases to reducing prices; wage increases in one trade or industry stimulate similar increases elsewhere; where wage increases exceed productivity growth, the difference takes the form of price increases. The rest follows once it is established as being generally true that those sectors where productivity is moving fastest set the pace, and that wage structures have an integrated pattern which preserves relativities. And this adds up to the proposition that the greater the acceleration in advanced productivity and with it in money earnings, the greater the gap between advanced and average productivity, and the greater the inflation, since the rise in real income is determined by average productivity and the rise in money income by the sectors leading in productivity increases.

The case is a formidable one. It rests on two propositions: first, that the pace is set by those leading sectors of industry where productivity is developing the fastest, and, second, that because of recognised relationships and comparabilities within and between industries, important changes in any parts of its structure will be reflected elsewhere in order to preserve the pattern. The former proposition is the less important in the sense that the wage increases need not be narrowly identified with productivity increases; the same result follows from what happens in any pacesetting sectors of industry, although it is reasonable to expect that such sectors will be ones where productivity increases are likely to be high (if only because expanding industries are likely to benefit from economies of scale). But it is the second proposition, that there is an element of interdependence in the wage pattern, that is essential to the argument. This seems to be the position in the U.K., where the Donovan Report* could be cited in evidence.

The authors can also cite further evidence from elsewhere† in confirmation or explanation of their argument. The collapse of the Dutch wage control system after 1960 following the attempt

---

* *Royal Commission on Trade Unions and Employers' Associations 1965-1968*, Cmnd. 3623 of 1968. See in particular paras. 57 to 59. Even the behaviour of earnings drift seems to emphasise the pattern.

† H. A. Turner and D. A. S. Jackson, 'On the Stability of Wage Differences and Productivity-based Wage Policies', *British Journal of Industrial Relations*, Vol. 7, No. 1, and H. A. Turner, 'Collective Bargaining and the Eclipse of Incomes Policy', *ibid.* Vol. 8, No. 2.

to impose a systematically-differentiated wage policy seems to confirm the brittle quality of an integrated wage structure with its established relativities. On the general issue they argue that economic analysis provides good reasons to explain why productivity increases in one sector should lead to wage movements in another: productivity implies increased substitution of machines thereby contributing to a general increase in real income; the income effect leads to an increased demand for labour in those parts of the economy where the demand for labour is inelastic since the possibility of substituting machines is less: i.e. growing richer one needs more men where machines will not do, and they too must have more pay. One expects the wage pressures to extend in response to the diffused demand for labour. (In the U.K. more demarcation disputes seem to illustrate this.)

But perhaps the most impressive confirmation of the Turner/ Jackson thesis as applying to advanced market economies is an oblique one. In underdeveloped economies – on the face of it the least likely – a similar process takes place: the industrial sectors pave the way and set the pace for wage increases. The existence of a large reserve of labour in the towns and the neighbouring countryside all available for employment does not prevent the upward movement of wages in the limited industrial sector.

Accepting this thesis, as on present evidence one cannot avoid doing, what are the implications? In the first place, it provides an inescapable argument against making productivity the centre of wage bargaining. The danger is that of concentrating the benefit of increased productivity on those most closely associated with the increase. Some concessions are needed to smooth the way and encourage changes in working arrangements, but these should not be on such a scale as largely to absorb the economies. The benefits must be diffused – for preference reflected in part in price reductions – if they are not to jack up money wages far beyond the level of average productivity increases. An effective prices and incomes policy must evolve round the average increase in productivity, and lean away from spectacular rewards for outstanding achievements.

The second conclusion is more general in character. It relates to the possibility of contracts made in terms of money payments being made adjustable in the light of movements in some agreed price index. A formula tying wage agreements directly to price changes could, on the face of it, have some effect in bringing wage claims down to a more reasonable level. But the widespread use of such devices in a wide range of contractual obligations would become unavoidable, and the risk would be run of an open-ended commitment. A formula which left wages rises no higher than the range of price increases could control inflation; but once bargaining took the form of maintaining purchasing power plus some further increase, there is no assurance that this further increase could be kept within the limits of average productivity, and once we get beyond the increase in G.D.P. the formula itself leads to an explosion: either an unlimited escalation in prices, or a redistribution of income within the community where gains in real terms are balanced by losses in real terms, which are unlikely to be acceptable to the losers.

The wage-fixing process is an illustration of what can happen when obligations are entered into on the basis of a formula which opens the way for rises which outrun the average increase of productivity. An accelerating upward movement of the price level will be set up. In this case the sequence will be – productivity leaders set the pace for wage increases; others follow on the basis of comparabilities and accepted differentials; wage level increases faster than average productivity; rises in consumer prices bridge the gap; employers try to cover increase in costs by cutting out redundant labour, thereby raising productivity; fresh rise in wage level to take advantage of productivity increase; again higher prices, more redundancies, and so on. Wage cost-push inflation leads to greater efficiency (up to a point) and unemployment through the shedding of labour in contrast to demand-pull inflation, which calls for more labour even at the risk of inefficiency; both are accompanied by rising prices and wages, but the former operates on a basis of contraction and labour-shedding, and the latter on labour absorption and expansion. If we push the contrast to its logical conclusion, in the case of cost push inflation the cumulative process is slowed down once a relaxation of pressure brings some stimulus to demand and enables the business to pass on its price increases without shedding redundant labour, and the extreme need for a smaller work force disappears. In the case of demand inflation the logical remedy is the opposite:

some fiscal constriction to moderate the demand, and perhaps some credit restriction to slow down any excessive expansion or wasteful use of labour.

But one clearly cannot leave the argument in this general state. What do we mean by productivity and by redundancy, and how far can they be said to overlap?

Productivity increases when a given volume of output can be produced by a lesser input of men and/or machines. In the simplest case, the same output is produced by the same machines, but by better arrangement the machines are efficiently looked after by fewer men. Here is a straightforward increase in productivity: there is a money saving in the first instance which can go to reducing prices, increasing wages, increasing profits – in full to any one of these, or in varying proportions. The saving is a saving on the wage bill, and (for the given output) some men will be redundant. If prices are reduced, or their rate of increase checked, there will be some increase in demand and a corresponding upward movement in employment, which will depend on the elasticity of demand. Redundancies may be absorbed. If all the saving goes in increased wages, there is no room for any reduction in prices and – assuming other things equal – the business goes on with the same output as before with fewer people employed, though those that remain have the higher wages. If it all goes in increased profits, a proportion of these profits may be ploughed back and invested in the business leading to expansion and efficiency in due course, but on the labour side there will be fewer workers, all with the same wage as before, while selling prices will be the same. It will be a matter for argument as to how the division should take place, but the example is a simple one since there is a visible saving to be divided.

But increased productivity may take a more complicated form, substituting machines for men. In this case there will be fewer men employed, but the saving from the reduction in the labour force will be needed, in part at any rate, to pay for the newer, more efficient, machinery. There will be some gain in overall productivity, one assumes, but it will be less than the saving in the wages which the redundant men would have earned. Such gain as there is may again be directed in varying proportions in the three directions, as in the earlier case.

In both the cases so far discussed there is at any rate some element of increased productivity, in the form of greater efficiency leading to some saving. But this does not exhaust the possibilities. What happens in the case of a straight fall in demand unaccompanied by any possibility of lowering costs? Or again, if there is no observable opportunity for effective productivity increases, but increased wage demands have to be met. In such cases the management will have to increase prices or to reduce the work force, or quite probably both. Increasing prices may mean reduced demand. Reducing the work force will mean a lower output (and possibly higher average costs if overheads have to be spread more narrowly). Either way there is a threat of redundancies without any productivity compensation. The problem of falling output leading to unavoidable increased costs engaged the attention of the Prices and Incomes Board.*

Even where there is no initial fall in demand, upward wage pressure in conditions of financial stringency can get beyond the point where increased productive efficiency is elicited, and the opposite tendency of decreasing average productivity per head may come in. Cutting back on the workers employed in order to limit the total wage bill may begin with a reduction in the quality of output, and beyond that it can get to the point where output has to be kept down to a level at which expensive plant may be unemployed. A cycle of higher wages – higher prices – fewer workers – higher overheads could create deteriorating conditions as menacing as those from too much money chasing too few goods, even though the mechanics of a cost push inflation and a demand inflation are different.

The Turner/Jackson argument explains the upward pressures of wages in a large number of countries over a considerable period of time (1956–65) but it is only a part of the story. Whether we treat it as different in kind or different in degree, the U.K. wages explosion of 1969/70 requires further explanation. From the middle 1950s to the later sixties, the annual rise in the U.K. cost of living averaged well under 4 per cent. The big jump, both in wages and in prices, comes from the middle of 1969 onwards; it was already in full swing by the time of the June 1970 election.

* As in the case of bricks. See J. F. Pickering, 'The Prices and Incomes Board and Private Sector Prices: a Survey' (*Economic Journal*, June 1971).

Nor is the U.K. alone in her difficulties, as the following table shows.

Six Leading Industrial Countries: Wages, Prices, Growth, Unemployment

| | Increase (per cent) 1970–71 | | | Unemployment (per cent) | |
	Wages	Consumer prices	G.N.P.	1969	1970
U.K.	12·0	8·9	0·4	3·7	3·9
U.S.A.	6·3	4·6	1·5	3·5	4·9
France	11·6	5·4	5·1	2·8	3·3
W. Germany	16·4	4·5	4·3	0·7	0·6
Italy	14·6	4·9	—	3·7	3·5
Japan	14·6	6·7	7·0	1·1	1·2

(Source: *National Institute Economic Review*, November 1971. The increases shown in the first three columns in effect represent the experience of the first half of 1971 as compared with the corresponding period in 1970. The unemployment percentages have been standardised for comparability. The U.K. unemployment figure is for G.B. only.)

It emerges that in respect of wage rises the U.K. has done considerably better than Italy, Germany and Japan. Nor is unemployment out of line with the other countries, excluding Germany and Japan where unemployment is negligible. Italy and Germany have had wage rises far exceeding the rise in G.N.P., (the provisional figures in the case of Italy's G.N.P. suggest that there was no rise and possibly a small fall) and it remains to be seen what the ultimate effect on consumer prices will be. In respect of the U.K. the question which stands out is: why is growth so low in spite of a large increase in wages?

For the rise in U.K. wages from the middle of 1969 onwards was unprecedented. The Bank for International Settlements* commenting on these rises, took the view that 'an important factor in the United Kingdom was discontent at the slower than usual advance of real wages in 1968–69.' How far can one build on such an explanation?

* *Annual Report* 1970–71.

The starting point must be to get some measure of the movements of the standard of living of the working population. To get an accurate picture we really need figures of take-home pay: the sum total of earnings less direct taxes and other deductions, revalued on a common price base. We have not got such a figure, but there are regular figures of 'personal disposable income at 1963 prices'. This adds together totals of wages and salaries; forces pay; employers' contribution to national insurance and pension funds; payments by public authorities in the form of national insurance benefits, family allowances, supplementary benefits etc.; and 'other personal income'. It then deducts income tax payments by persons and national insurance and similar contributions. The resulting total is not quite what one wants because of the inclusion of the other personal income – how important this is will be discussed later – but it does give us a picture of personal spending power after payments in respect of direct taxes have been subtracted. The table which follows compares changes in the total of real personal disposable income with changes in G.D.P. at constant prices; both columns are on the basis of 1963 prices.

Changes in Disposable Income and Gross Domestic Product
(at constant 1963 prices)

	Increase in personal disposable income %	Increase in G.D.P. %
1964–7	6·2	6·3
1967–68	1·9	3·6
1968–69	0·9	2·0
1969–70	3·4	1·7
1970–71	0·2	0·9

(Source: *Economic Trends* and *Monthly Statistics*.)

Before examining the figures, we must ask ourselves how far the inclusion of 'other personal income' could affect the figures and their significance as a measure of living standards of the working population. The figure comprises income from self-employment, income from rent and dividend and interest receipts.

This accounts for about a fifth of the total gross, but must be expected to carry a more than proportionate weight of taxation. In sum: if we are concerned with narrow movements of the figures, it could have an effect, but if the movements are large and clearly marked it should not disturb conclusions to be drawn from them.

The movements of the figures are clearly marked. From 1964 to 1967, in real terms increase in disposable income and in G.D.P. kept pace with each other (though one must not forget the wage freeze in 1966 and devalution coming at the end of 1967). From 1967 to 1968 increase in disposable income continued but G.D.P. increased at twice that rate. Between 1968 and 1969 the increase in disposable income halved; increase in G.D.P. also fell, but still was twice as much as that of disposable income. The pressure was too much, and triggered off the wages explosion. Real disposable income went right up and jumped to twice that of G.D.P. The wage earner can recall that a wages freeze was accepted in 1966; great moderation had been shown after devaluation; up to 1969 the increase in living standards had been minimal. Now that the balance of payments problem had been brought under control, it was time for some effective concession on living standards. Moreover, this was not just the due reward for restraint, it was an economic necessity, for there was a smell of unemployment in the air, and the remedy for unemployment (one is told) is expansion through increasing effective demand, and this was now possible with workers and resources unused and available.

That is how it looks to the wage earner. He must be concerned above all to protect his standard of living. He is familiar with rising prices. He may have heard that increased taxes by slowing down spending power will help to keep prices down, but his experience contradicts this. For him, higher taxes and decreased government expenditure directly contribute to higher prices: indirect taxes are passed on and are meant to be passed on; 'savings' on government expenditure mean that rents go up; people have to pay for medicines and school milk and meals and museums, which they have been getting for little or nothing, and still more for power and transport and the post, for which they are already paying a lot. The public feels that an increased budget surplus means an increased cost of living, and it adjusts its way of bargaining accordingly. This is not surprising: experience confirms them in this view, and the steps thought to be required to make us eligible for the Common Market do not help persuade them otherwise. Finally, increasing unemployment has made them aware that the economy is not being worked to its full capacity: there are unused resources which leave room for expansion. And so we as wage earners fight to protect (and seek to raise) our standard of living.

The figures examined so far are in terms of averages, and averages conceal grievances. It is not enough to show that an average increase of a moderate amount should be sufficient to maintain the standard of living. If the margin is at all narrow, there are bound to be some who do suffer a fall, while others are gainers to a more than normal extent. This applies as between occupations. It also applies to different income levels: in particular the loss of social security benefits on the one hand and the incidence of taxes on the other, bears especially hardly at particular levels of remuneration. In the case of the lower paid there is a point where an increase in pay could mean an appreciable fall in real income, because it coincides with the level of eligibility for various social security and related benefits. A similar effect arises rather higher up in the income scale, where the weight of income tax begins to press. Once an increasing number of benefits and concessions is made subject to a means test this will enlarge the number of those who face a rise in pay in the knowledge that it means a withdrawal of remunerative privileges, and they look for a further compensating rise accordingly.

There are instructive examples of what happens when one looks at cases. An article in *New Society** takes the case of the median wage-earner (married with two children). On these figures between 1959–64 gross money income increased annually by 5.6 per cent, and net real income by 1.9 per cent. The corresponding figures for 1964–69 are 7.1 per cent and 1.0 per cent. (The rise between 1969 and 1970 is estimated at 11.9 per cent and 2.7 per cent respectively). Again the low average increases before 1969 conceals the fact that for some groups of workers – local government manual workers and electricity workers are instances –

---

* H. A. Turner and Frank Wilkinson, 'Real Net Incomes and the Wage Explosion', *New Society*, 25 February 1971.

there was no increase over the period or even a fall. 'The 1970 wage explosion may well represent, therefore, one of frustrated – but perhaps not altogether unjustified – expectations.'

Another article* deals with the question of deductions in the context of current government proposals for rent rebates and the Family Income Supplement. If these came into effect as proposed they will have an uneven incidence for particular groups. In particular the low paid – those earning between £10 and £15 – will be very hard hit; when they receive a pay rise to compensate for the cost of living they will see the social benefits decrease while their insurance contributions go up.

Above this the next range where difficulties arise is in the £20 to £30 per week group, where income tax begins to bite. Here to balance an 8 per cent increase in the cost of living an increase of over 12 per cent will be required to maintain real income. Higher up in the income scale as some deductions are stabilised and spread over a larger income the increase tails off: for those earning between £40 and £50 per week an 8 per cent increase in gross earnings should keep pace with an 8 per cent increase in the cost of living.

But to focus attention on the relationship between the rise in gross money income and net real income is to distract attention from a wider issue: that of wage bargaining and the general level of unemployment. Here by 1969 a new force was making itself felt: the fear of unemployment and a growing sense of insecurity.

The conventional view of these matters – the philosophy of the Phillips curve – has had to be discarded. One cannot assume the existence of a given level of unemployment – not too intolerable – which will have a stabilising effect on wages and prices; such calculations are too rational to be relevant. Many industrial disputes show evidence of fear and irrationality. The revolution in the docks is one case. New methods – in particular the growth of container traffic – open the way for simpler and more efficient working with a lower labour force. They also change the balance between the various ports. Even if there is room for substantially higher wages, there may be conflicts of interest which reinforce

---

* Peter Kellner, 'Why fair rents will bring giant wage demands', *Sunday Times*, 18 July 1971. See also the figures given in the *Trades Union Congress Economic Review 1972* (paragraphs 163–6) on this problem.

resistance to the phased and compensated reduction in the work force which should go with the change. The consequence is a confused conflict with no one the winners and damage inflicted all round. The same thing with the motor industry and with its ancillary suppliers – conflict and damage undermining otherwise not unsatisfactory prospects. And so also in engineering and elsewhere: an element of fear that this is the last chance to make a satisfactory bargain, and that as time goes on bargaining power will be lost. May it not be that the prospect of unemployment stimulates resistance rather than acceptance?

Some of these forces are at work in other countries: automation, the displacement of labour by machines, is a prospect in many places. But the difference is that in the U.K. the possibility of growth seems smaller, and perhaps the process of readjustment more difficult. That is what gives the position in this country its peculiar flavour. Elsewhere, the possibility of more rapid growth may make it just that much easier for both sides of industry to reach a common basis of policy of advantage to both.

If fear of unemployment and insecurity, coupled with indifferent prospects for compensating growth, are the driving force in the demand for higher wages before bargaining prospects deteriorate, the economic arguments for such a course are not negligible. Once it is conceded that there are workpeople available together with unused capacity, an increase in spending power should lead to more employment and more output, and this in its turn should increase the supply of goods and services and so moderate the rise in prices. Is it suggested that by keeping wages pegged more people will be employed or more factories turning over faster? Indeed, the case for some reflation has been conceded, and if so more money in the workers' pockets is as likely to be effective as anything. But how much more? No one is in a hurry to answer.

If much of this has force, much of it also is shadow-boxing. Of course what we are really talking about is an acceptable and agreed prices and incomes and growth policy, which will provide reassurance to workers and industry and give a prospect of stable development. It is not possible to make redundancy acceptable, or even to persuade people to accept it as unavoidable, unless and until they can be persuaded that there are new developments which will offer employment to them. A vision of these is still lacking. The basis of an acceptable incomes and prices policy must be an assurance that new opportunities will replace those that have disappeared because of technical progress and improved organisation.

7. *Reversal Points*

We have been dealing with methods and policy instruments at the disposal of the community for certain desirable ends: that the standard of living should be increased; that purchasing power should not be eroded; that a high and continuous level of employment should be maintained; that we should pay our way in our dealings with other countries; that we should have a wage structure which can be shown to be fair and equitable, and acceptable accordingly. The pursuit of these ends gives rise to problems, and a balance has to be kept between them. Over recent years the main problem has been that of keeping the economy from overheating; hence the emphasis on pressure. But we cannot assume that the difficulties will continue in their present shape. In times past the problem has been the opposite: that of providing a stimulus. In the future that could be the problem again. But at all times one must be on the look-out for turning points, when above all there is the necessity of keeping a balance between control and stimulus.

The basic methods at our disposal have been fiscal and credit pressure. These methods, in conjunction with others, have been used to produce at a further stage certain consequential pressures: related to employment, to export, to wage bargaining. In simple terms, we control spending power and financial facilities in order to avoid excessive pressure on the labour market, in order to secure an adequate volume of exports, in order to prevent a competitive rise of wages and of other prices. The basic pressure over the years leading up to 1971 has been intense; the results have been mixed and in some respects very unhappy. Against a very impressive improvement in our balance of payments we have to show negligible economic growth, sensational rises in the cost of living and in wages, and a serious threat of growing unemployment. It is perhaps some consolation that we are not alone in this.

So far much has been said about methods and mechanics –

the tools at our disposal. Less has been said about the way that we are using them.

The argument now to be put forward is that in respect of all these methods there are certain points beyond which each of them not only becomes useless but dangerous – having an opposite effect to that intended. A medicine taken to excess is no longer providing a remedy; it is making the patient very much worse. What is now suggested is that in respect of all these policies – whether relating to net government spending, or credit, or employment, or exports, or wage bargaining, there is a reversal point beyond which, once it is reached, the carrying further of the policy will be damaging and frustrate its own ends. It is further suggested that in each case it should be possible to identify this reversal point, where the policy becomes self-defeating. We take them in turn.

Fiscal policy. The reversal point had clearly been passed by the second half of 1970, when the subject had broken into the correspondence columns of *The Times*. Thus Sir Roy Harrod* on the Budget surplus:

'I believe that many people do not appreciate that this is something absolutely fabulous, out-of-this-world, many times as great as this country, or any other, has ever seen before. It was £2,444 million last year, and £2,598 million is planned for 1970-71. Translating into American terms, it means that our taxpayers are having to find for the Budget surplus, that is for nothing at all, more than two thirds of what American taxpayers have to find for their huge defence expenditures at home and abroad.

I am confident that this Budget surplus has been the main cause of the wages explosion that we have recently had, which is said to be going to continue. The exorbitant taxation pushes up prices and the cost of living.'

This theme was taken up again early in the next year by Sir John Walley (formerly of the Ministry of Social Security). Discussing the increasing size of wage settlements he wrote:

'I suggest that the initial impetus has come from pressures

* *The Times*, 14 August 1970.

on lower paid married men with families whose plight enlists public sympathy and makes employers less inclined to resist. This was recognised in the war by the Churchill Government's concord with the T.U.C. in family allowances, with subsidised food prices and the promise of free school meals and milk. It was recognised again by Churchill's Conservative Government in 1952 when their abolition of the bread subsidy was accompanied by a 60 per cent increase of family allowances and of child tax-allowances as well.

How striking is the contrast today'.*

He went on to make the point that the favourable effect of an increase in family allowances had been destroyed because it had been linked

'with a further attack on cheap school meals, etc., and then by the 'clawback' from the child tax-allowance, which deprived the standard rate taxpayer of even the small benefit he had expected from the increase.'

To this had to be added other examples, including the abolition of lower initial tax rates and a disproportionate share in the big increases of flat rate National Insurance contributions. Finally, with the new government there were the heavy increased charges on school meals and milk.

Arguments such as these gain their force from the way they illuminate a situation in which the rise in prices was to reach a rate of 10 per cent per annum. Sir Roy Harrod concluded his letter:

'I suppose that there are some who believe that a Budget surplus is an anti-inflationary weapon. This idea is correct in wartime or on other occasions when the total demand for goods and services is running above the supply potential of the economy. It is entirely false in relation to our existing situation. At the present time the Budget surplus is strongly inflationary.'

These letters have been quoted at this length not only because of their substance but because of their timing; they show that by 1970 responsible observers are already calling attention to the

* *The Times*, 20 January 1971.

dangers of a policy which has been pushed so far that it has passed what we are calling its reversal point, and is back-firing. With the evidence we have after the event, is it possible to maintain that if the increase in taxation had been a little more moderate the rise in prices would have been any greater? Or if taxation had been a little greater, the rise in prices any less? This is the test which suggests that the point of reversal had long been passed; the dose was excessive and the medicine was putting the patient in peril. The question that needed to be asked all along was how far could taxation have been increased without provoking a more powerful counter effect.

Credit policy. The danger of excessive squeeze in this country was tempered by investment allowances or grants and other incentives, and this was the deliberate policy of both parties. It could perhaps be argued that given the weight of fiscal pressure, investment grants could not make very much difference. But even if this is so, it is all the more important that as fiscal pressure is relaxed a corresponding easement is made on the credit side, so that as demand increases there is the necessary encouragement for expanding output. Tightening of credit policy has implications for investment from the very beginning. But it really starts holding up output once there is a potential demand for output with an easing of fiscal pressure. It is at that point that incentives for investment and expansion are most needed.

Employment policy. In the case of unemployment above all, one can find an exceptionally clear example of a reversal point, when the unemployment situation changes completely in character. While unemployment is relatively low one is still in the position of having side by side areas where unemployment is beginning to become serious and other areas where demand continues and jobs are available. At this stage the disparities of employment offer opportunities for adjustment; men can move from the bad areas to the prosperous ones. One still has the chance of making progress with sensible policies as long as there is nothing to prevent movements of labour from areas of growing unemployment to areas where work is available and men are needed.

The matter is quite different – in kind and not only in degree – once unemployment becomes general. It is not just the size of unemployment, but its spread. In the age of unemployment between the two wars there was little point in an unemployed man going from say South Wales, fantastically high though the unemployment in his home town might be, on the off chance of finding better opportunities in the Midlands or in London. The reversal point comes when there are no longer places where newcomers are welcome.

Even moderate unemployment in potential receiving areas become a major deterrent to labour coming in from outside; the test is whether there are more than enough local men to fill any likely jobs. This is the reversal point: when unemployment is becoming general in character. Contrasting employment prospects, even if in some places the unemployment is heavy, leave room for movements of labour and scope for adjustment. When unemployment is spreading over the whole country – though in parts still lightly – then the mobility of labour becomes seriously reduced. The test is the flow of people between different areas in search of work. The critical point, the signal for drastic action, is when the immobilisation of the labour force starts to increase, and real danger threatens.

Export policy. Under foreign pressure – and with foreign help – the U.K. turned a substantial deficit on her current balance of payments in 1967 and 1968 into an even more substantial surplus in 1969, 1970 and 1971. This at any rate is an achievement for which the strategy of financial pressure must be given credit. But again one must ask whether it might not have been better to proceed more slowly in our efforts to improve our balance of payments positions. An improved balance on international account means that we are selling more of our own output abroad, and/or buying less from abroad. In one or both of these two ways we are subtracting potential supplies which otherwise would have been available for the domestic market. Further, we are running down stocks and skimping capital re-equipment. Hence the warning: 'Your very success in that one branch of policy, getting the balance of payments right, is going to cause you to have more trouble in another branch of your policy – getting the movement of the price level under control'* One need not question the direction of the policy, but we have to ask: had we gone more slowly,

* Professor E. Caves, of Harvard, quoted in the *Financial Times*, 11 April 1970.

and not proceeded so far and so fast, would not some of the other consequences which have been damaging us have been less serious?

Wage bargaining policy. Excessive emphasis on increased productivity as a justification for higher wages has been leading us very near to the position that the more productivity goes up the faster the rate of inflation. This at any rate seems to be the moral of the formidable argument put up by Professor Turner and Mr Jackson, that the rate of wage rises the world over are dictated by those sectors where productivity is rising fastest, while price stability requires wage increases which do not exceed the average rising in productivity in the economy as a whole. A particular negotiating approach of some merit – some inducements are needed to ease the transition to new and more effective working arrangements and practices – has been pushed beyond its reasonable limits and turned into a basis for distributing rewards, with the results that have been noted.

The theme that has been argued is that in each of these spheres of policy – fiscal and credit; unemployment, export and wage bargaining – there are limits to go beyond which puts the intended effects into reverse. These limits, be it noted, are not independent of each other. In the case of fiscal policy, the limit is reached as soon as people are convinced that an increase in taxation is going to increase (and not reduce) prices, and react accordingly. (And it should be added that the limit is reached more quickly if the methods of increasing taxation appear unfair, maladroit or unimaginative; it is instructive to read Keynes' *How to Pay for the War* to see how delicately he handles the question of making necessary taxation fair and acceptable.)

In the case of credit policy, there is from the beginning a constraining element in its effect on industrial expansion. This may matter less when fiscal constraint is in any case reducing the scope for expansion, especially if alleviations are being applied to prevent credit policy biting too harshly. But the moment that there is some relaxation of fiscal policy and demand begins to rise, credit policy becomes very material as any witholding of facilities may throttle the expansion which the increased demand is intended to elicit.

In the case of employment policy – we have not yet reached

this reversal point – there is the danger of an element of general unemployment which would spread over the country and blanket the mobility of labour. In the case of exports the danger is that of moving too far and too fast, so that the very success of the policy denudes the home market of potential supplies and so sets in motion forces which could in the end destroy the very purpose the policy was meant to achieve. Lastly, wage bargaining suffers the blows which come its way when other policies miscarry, but over-emphasis on productivity has brought its own difficulties.

This examination of the instruments of financial policy and their uses cannot claim to have produced very reassuring results. A critic might assert that over the last seven years financial policy instead of stabilising prices has blown them sky high, and instead of stimulating growth has killed it stone dead. But this is going too far; after all, we have maintained full and continuous employment and a steady if modest rise in our standard of living over a long period of time, and the developments which we failed to foresee and which are pressing not only upon us but on other developed countries in the world are not such as to be dealt with by financial policy alone. Nevertheless we have not been very clever. Perhaps two of the lessons we most need to remember is that policies pursued too far and/or too fast turn against us, and that it is important to use the instruments at our disposal in concert and in concord with each other.

CHAPTER THREE

U.K. Experience 1962-72: Spending, Profits and Liquidity

What follows is concerned with analysing the evidence available on the overall position of the company and personal sectors as things have developed over the last ten years, and more particularly since 1965. The basic information has been arranged in the form of half-a-dozen tables. What appears to emerge is that personal spending and saving have continued at a reasonable and uninterrupted level, modestly increasing in real terms, but that in addition the liquidity position has been further reinforced by switches of assets. In contrast, the liquidity of the company sector has been very seriously reduced, possibly to the extent of damaging its capacity for expansion should effective demand be allowed to increase.

The rest of this chapter is taken up with a discussion of the implications of this.

1. *Company Profitability and Liquidity*

The position of all companies from 1962 to 1971 is summarised in Table A. This shows income divided under three heads: gross trading profits in the U.K. (the basic item); rent and non-trading income; and income from abroad (this item being netted, income paid out abroad being subtracted from receipts and not shown as an outgoing). The total arrived at is split under four heads: dividends on ordinary shares; other dividends and interest; U.K. taxes on income; (the residual balance) undistributed income. It should be noted that in this table additions to tax reserves have been included with tax payments and not under undistributed income.

Table A   U.K. Companies: Income and Allocation 1962–71

(£ thousand million)

	1962	1963	1964	1965	1966	1967	1968	1969	1970	1971
Gross trading profits in U.K.	3·6	4·1	4·6	4·8	4·4	4·6	5·0	5·0	5·0	5·8
Rent and non-trading income	0·9	0·9	1·1	1·2	1·4	1·5	1·7	1·9	2·1	2·4
Income from abroad (net)	0·5	0·5	0·5	0·6	0·6	0·6	0·7	0·9	0·9	0·8
Total income for allocation (including miscellaneous items)	5·0	5·5	6·2	6·6	6·4	6·7	7·3	7·8	8·0	9·0
Dividends on Ordinary shares	1·2	1·3	1·5	1·7	1·7	1·6	1·6	1·8	1·7	1·7
Other dividends, interest, etc.	0·6	0·7	0·8	0·9	1·1	1·3	1·5	1·7	1·8	1·9
U.K. taxes on income (and additions to tax reserves)	0·8	0·8	1·0	0·7	1·2	1·3	1·6	1·7	1·5	1·3
Balance: undistributed income after taxation	2·3	2·6	2·8	3·3	2·4	2·6	2·5	2·7	3·0	4·0

(Source: *National Income and Expenditure, 1971* and *Preliminary Estimates of the National Income and Balance of Payments 1966–1971*, Cmnd. 4935 of 1972)

The top line of table A shows the basic element of trading profits rising in the first two years – a period of credit relaxation. After 1964 there is little rise. 1967 is no better than 1964, but there is some increase in 1968 and an appreciable increase in 1971. These figures are in terms of current prices in a period when prices were going up. The retail price index (January 1962 = 100) was up to 147 and 159 in January 1971 and 1972 respectively. The imprint of deflationary pressure is unmistakable in the case of trading profits. However, with the rising cost of finance, rent and non-trading income double, and net income from abroad almost does the same, with the help from devaluation. In the outcome, total income available for allocation keeps up with rising prices.

The allocation repeats the pattern. Dividends on Ordinary shares are no higher in 1970 than in 1965, but the cost of other borrowing and interest has doubled, with higher interest rates and increased borrowing constraints. U.K. taxes have also doubled. The undistributed balance – needed for keeping capital intact, for stock appreciation, as well as for possible expansion – shows a history even more discouraging than that of the trading profits. Only in 1971 is there noticeable improvement.

The next stage is to trace through the relationship between the undistributed income and investment. Table B differs from

Table B   Industrial and Commercial Companies: Undistributed Income and Capital Expenditure

(£ thousand million)

	1 Undistributed Income	2 Capital Formation	3 Stocks	4 Excess of Capital Expenditure (2+3−1)
1965	3·0	2·4	0·6	—
1966	2·7	2·4	0·4	0·1
1967	2·7	2·3	0·2	−0·2
1968	3·0	2·5	0·7	0·2
1969	3·0	2·8	1·1	0·9
1970	2·7	3·2	1·1	1·6
1971	3·5	3·3	0·6	−0·4

(Source: *Financial Statistics*)

Table C Industrial and Commercial Companies: Selected Liquid Assets
(£ thousand million)

Amount outstanding at end of	1962	1963	1964	1965	1966	1967	1968	1969	1970	1971
Treasury bills, tax reserve certificates and local authority temporary debt	1·0	1·1	1·0	0·8	0·7	0·7	0·6	0·5	0·4	0·5
Deposits with building societies and finance houses	0·2	0·2	0·3	0·3	0·3	0·3	0·3	0·4	0·4	0·4
Deposits with banking sector:										
Deposit banks	2·2	2·0	2·0	2·1	2·0	2·1	2·2	1·9	2·1	2·4
Others		0·6	0·6	0·7	0·9	1·1	1·4	1·5	1·7	2·3
Total identified	3·5	3·9	3·9	3·9	3·8	4·3	4·5	4·3	4·5	5·7
less Bank advances Deposit banks	−2·4	−2·4	−2·7	−3·0	−3·2	−3·2	−3·4	−3·7	−3·9	−3·8
Other		−0·4	−0·6	−0·8	−0·8	−1·0	−1·2	−1·4	−2·0	−2·6
Net total	1·1	1·1	0·6	0·1	−0·2	0·1	−0·1	−0·7	−1·4	−0·8
Change on preceding year		—	−0·5	−0·5	−0·3	0·3	−0·2	−0·6	−0·7	0·6

(Source: *Financial Statistics*)

table A in that it covers industrial and commercial companies only, with financial companies excluded. There is also a difference in definition of undistributed income, in that additions to tax reserves are included.

It will be noted that – in spite of rising prices – undistributed income is lower in 1970 than in 1965, while capital expenditure (which includes replacement) has inevitably increased. However the table does not include investment grants, which provided ·2 in 1967, ·4 in 1968, ·6 in 1969, ·5 in 1970, ·5 in 1971. Even allowing for this, the position leaves little scope for expansion. Investment grants of a general character have since been abolished. Stocks are affected by rising prices.

The changing liquidity position is shown in table C.

The overall liquidity position of industrial and commercial companies taken as a whole has deteriorated spectacularly. A surplus of liquid assets of over £1,000 million in 1962 and 1963 has changed to a deficiency which reaches a peak of £1,400 million in 1970. In 1962 and 1963 the net amount owed to the banking system after subtracting deposits from advances was £200 million. In 1970 it had risen to over £2,000 million.

In contrast, in 1971 there is a major turn-round. Instead of deterioration, there is appreciable improvement. But this is the year of financial relaxation and special factors come in; with prices still rising, it cannot be assumed that improvement on such a scale will continue. We are still left with an industrial and commercial sector with depleted resources, and it would be unwise to rely on its being able to finance a large and sudden increase in output when it is faced with a big jump in demand.

2. *Persons: Spending, Saving and Liquidity*

The personal sector has followed a different course from that of the company sector. Table D shows (1) Personal disposable income: that is, total income less income taxes, contributions and payments abroad; (2) Consumers' expenditure at market prices; (3) Personal savings, which is the balance after subtracting expenditure from disposable income, and (4) Personal saving as a percentage of disposable income.

Table D   Persons: Disposable Income, Expenditure and Savings

(£ *thousand million*)

	1 Disposable Income	2 Consumers' Expenditure	3 Personal Saving	(%) 4 Saving as % of Income
1965	25·0	22·9	2·1	8·3
1966	26·5	24·3	2·2	8·3
1967	27·7	25·4	2·2	8·0
1968	29·5	27·2	2·3	7·8
1969	31·2	28·8	2·5	7·9
1970	34·0	31·2	2·8	8·2
1971	37·5	34·5	3·0	8·0

(Source: *Financial Statistics*)

Thus from 1965 to 1971, disposable income in money terms increased in all by 50 per cent. It should be added that in real terms the increase in consumption was about 10 per cent. At any rate the personal sector had a more comfortable journey than the company sector without anything very alarming happening.

A comparison of table E with the corresponding table C for the company sector shows a complete contrast. Company liquidity slides into the red; the personal sector is building up its liquid assets by well over £1,000 million each year. Personal borrowing from the banks does not increase; personal sector bank deposits do. Above all there is an increase of £7,000 million in deposits with building societies over the years 1965–71. (This item is almost entirely building societies; the finance house element is small).

Table F sets (1) Personal Saving (as in Table D) alongside (2) Life and Superannuation funds investment and (3) Increase in liquid assets (as in table E). (4) shows sales of Company securities etc. The last column adds savings and proceeds of sales and subtracts the expenditure on life assurance and pensions and the build-up of liquid assets. Over the seven years the personal sector used its unspent disposable income (totalling £17,100 million) in making life and superannuation fund payments (to the tune

Table E Personal Sector: Selected Liquid Assets
(£ thousand million)

Amount outstanding at end of	1962	1963	1964	1965	1966	1967	1968	1969	1970	1971
National savings, tax reserve certificates and local authority temporary debt	7·7	8·0	8·5	8·6	8·6	8·7	8·9	8·8	8·9	9·5
Deposits with building societies and finance houses	3·5	4·0	4·5	5·2	5·9	7·0	7·8	8·7	10·2	12·1
Deposits with banking sector:										
Deposit banks	5·9	6·1	6·5	6·9	7·2	7·8	8·4	8·6	9·3	10·3
Others		0·2	0·3	0·3	0·3	0·4	0·6	0·6	0·7	0·8
Total identified	17·0	18·2	19·7	21·1	22·0	24·0	25·6	26·7	29·1	32·6
less Bank advances										
Deposit banks	−1·7	−1·7	−1·9	−1·8	−1·7	−1·9	−1·9	−1·8	−1·8	−2·3
Others		−0·1	−0·1	−0·1	−0·1	−0·1	−0·2	−0·1	−0·2	−0·2
Net total	15·3	16·4	17·7	19·2	20·2	22·0	23·5	24·8	27·1	30·1
Change on preceding year (increase)		1·1	1·3	1·5	1·0	1·8	1·5	1·3	2·3	3·0

(Source: Financial Statistics)

Table F   *Personal Savings 1965–1970*
(£ *thousand million*)

	1 Personal Saving	2 Life and Super- annuation Funds	3 Increase in Liquid Assets	4 Sales of Company Securities	5 Net balance: (1+4) less (2+3)
1965	2·1	1·2	1·5	0·6	0·0
1966	2·2	1·2	1·0	0·4	0·4
1967	2·2	1·4	1·8	0·5	−0·5
1968	2·3	1·5	1·5	0·4	−0·3
1969	2·5	1·5	1·3	0·4	0·1
1970	2·8	1·8	2·3	0·8	−0·5
1971	3·0	2·0	3·0	1·2	−0·8
Total	17·1	10·6	12·4	4·3	−1·6

(Source: *Financial Statistics*. The figures in cols. 1 and 3 are those which appear in tables D and E above.)

of £10,600 million) and increasing liquid assets (£12,400 million). At the same time there was selling of investments in the company sector (£4,300 million).

The personal sector has been prosperous compared to the company sector.

3. *Interpretation and Implications*

Personal liquid assets increased between 1962 and 1970 from £15,300 million to £27,100 million, an increase of 77 per cent.

Over the same period National Income increased by 65 per cent in money terms (though only by 22 per cent in real terms).

Industrial and commercial companies' liquid assets fell from a surplus of £1,000 million to a deficiency of £1,400 million.

How is all this to be explained?

To put it at its lowest, it is unexpected. With rising prices – and prices were rising with a sharp acceleration towards the end of the period – one might have expected increased demand to be reflected in increased profits. This is not the case. From 1965 gross trading profits of all companies (before deducting taxes and distributions) are more or less stationary in money terms and heavily down in real terms. Other increased revenues about match increased taxation and interest payments. But equity dividends and undistributed income are again stationary in money terms and down in real terms. Finally, the industrial and commercial sector is hardly in a fit state to meet any sharp increase in effective demand, even though there is labour and capacity at its disposal; there is no assurance that it will have – or be in a position to secure – the necessary working capital to meet the needed increase in the wages bill or in the bill for added materials and components, except in so far as over time the build up of retained profits may hold the position.

The pressure on the company sector is seen most clearly in three items. Stagnation in gross trading shows that the profit margin has been squeezed in real terms; with rising costs prices have not risen in proportion. (This would seem to be confirmed by the doubling of rent and non-trading income, where wage and similar costs would be less important.) Next the financial out-payments on interest etc. have risen, the consequences of tight money conditions arising from the credit squeeze. Last, taxes on income are heavily up, the fiscal squeeze. Financial pressure seems to have had its effect, not just in reducing the possibility of expansion, but in making the continuation of business difficult. It has not succeeded in keeping down costs, and as we know wages have been rising in spite of the pressure. (The position here being discussed is that up to 1970, before the thaw in 1971.)

In such conditions it is equally surprising to find how undisturbed the personal sector appears to be. Disposable income (after tax) goes on rising; the proportion saved continues at around 8 per cent; but above all the increase in liquid assets continues year after year. The savings pattern is significant: liquid assets, and life and superannuation funds built up in excess of current saving, and the balance made good largely by sales of company securities. The individual saver is preferring to see his money with a building society (where there is a tax concession) rather than in equities, which he is selling (presumably) to the managers of insurance and pension funds who can afford to wait.

This seems understandable enough – except that it is happening in a period of rising prices. This is the unintended miracle of rising prices and rising unemployment at the same time.

An undiscriminating use of the economic and financial weapons in our armoury has taken us up to and beyond the point where increasing taxation is immediately reflected in rising prices, while the squeeze on both the cost and availability of credit has put in doubt not only the capacity of the company sector to expand output where opportunity offers but even to maintain output at a short-run optimal level. That is, profitable business may have to be forgone on account of shortage of finance. Further, rising prices are making the shortage of liquidity worse as they reinforce rising costs, in particular wage costs. The view that if companies are kept short of liquidity they will be unable to concede overgenerous wage settlements does not eliminate the possibility that if carried to excess this shortage of liquidity will equally prevent them from undertaking expansion where expansion is profitable, and indeed possibly even hamper their continuing at their normal level of output.

The liquidity position of the personal sector is far from suggesting that there is yet any danger of an excess of demand leading to inflationary effects; it is from the supply side that the anxieties come. An expansion of demand in the ordinary way would be expected to lead to an increase in supply made possible through increasing profits and increasing liquidity. This has not been happening. Financial pressure has failed to stop the increase in prices, and succeeded in stopping investment. In the last resort if this was to continue unchecked, the weakness of the company sector could in due course work back on the personal sector and induce (with the help of rising prices) a movement out of liquid assets into goods.

More immediately, the vital increase in effective demand which we need could find itself faced by a failure of output to rise owing to monetary constraints, so that developments which were intended to stop prices rising have the opposite effect of forcing up prices because increasing money demand is not being met by increasing supplies of goods.

Is this picture overdrawn? What is to be done?

One hopes that the picture is overdrawn. It can be said at once that if the pace of any increase in demand is moderate, and builds up over a period of time and is accompanied by liberal lending by the banks coupled with an increasing flow of income in due course reinforcing cash flow and profits, then the position could be viewed with less anxiety. But are we prepared to put our money on such a process of protracted destagnation? Surely we are more likely to be faced with a rush of demand – perhaps all the more intense if it is some time in coming – which raises the issues acutely. However much we may hope that the picture is overdrawn, it is consistent with the figures and with the known facts, and if it is over-stated in degree, that does not dispose of the analysis put forward, or of the basic problem of rising prices, or the contrasts inherent in the figures.

So, assuming for the sake of argument that the problem posed exists even if it is over-stated, what is to be done?

In the first place, we can agree credit relaxation must keep pace with increases in effective demand; there is substantial unused capacity in the economy which if it could be brought into operation could make a contribution in keeping down prices through increased output. The two processes require careful co-ordination.

Second, the gross trading profits of companies increased between 1965 and 1970 by under 10 per cent over the whole period. The gross trading profits of public corporations increased by very much more. Perhaps a slower rate of increase in public sector pricing as well as in private sector wage policy would have been expedient. This has a moral for the future given the desirability – and inevitability? – of an agreed policy on wage settlements between the two sides of industry.

Third, if as may be the case, the analysis of the position set out here turns out not to have been so greatly overdrawn (and the facts should soon make themselves apparent) we need to think in terms of the injection of funds into the company sector, perhaps through the provision of finance on an interest-free basis in the first instance (the finance being chargeable or repayable as liquidity returns). This would mean a direct stimulus to accelerated production over and above the considerable measures which have followed since the 1971 thaw. But this is a part of a wider field which needs more thorough exploration.

CHAPTER FOUR

The Scope and Limitations of Financial Action

1. *The Limitations*

The purpose of this chapter is to make, on the basis of the foregoing analysis, some assessment of the scope for financial action and of the obstacles to be avoided or overcome. It is a matter of implications rather than of conclusions.

The field of action is restricted in three directions: as it were, by three boundaries whose existence one is compelled to recognise. In the first place we must assume at the least some working understanding in respect of prices and incomes; one can conduct an effective financial policy only within some such framework. One would hazard that such a framework would have to cover in addition to prices and incomes, understandings about policy on employment and growth as well. Second, one has to take account of the fact that each of the instruments of policy has built in limitations so that it reaches a reversal point after which it becomes counter-productive, and destroys what it is intended to achieve. We have to consider not only what we want to do, but to what extent it is sensible to do it: in other words, we not only prescribe the medicine but have to prescribe the dose. The third point – a main theme of this study – is frequently overlooked in discussion and it could be in policy making also. We have so much to say about the importance of effective demand that we overlook effective supply, and its dependence on adequate finance. Stocks need to be larger, unused capacity has to be made ready and added to, when production goes up. It could be easy to stimulate money demand, but if the response is not quick enough we get a rise in prices instead of the increase in output and employ-

ment for which we are working, and a rise in imports of goods
we could produce for ourselves.

These points in themselves are all relatively simple, except for
the anxious complexities to which they give rise; they do restrict
the field of action considerably, and one must say something
about each.

First, what is described above as some working understanding on prices and incomes. One must be prepared for this to fall
short of a formally agreed or accepted policy, for one cannot
expect people to commit themselves in advance when much of
the detail has to be worked out in the light of experience. Impelled
by sense and self-interest people could come to act in accordance
with a policy, without any overt and formal commitment. An
understanding may be as much as one can hope for.

But such an understanding would have to be comprehensive.
It will not be enough to think in terms of money wages in isolation, when the real wages are what people are concerned with;
and this at once brings in prices and the standard of living. And
pricing may raise problems on its own account. If some prices
have remained too low for too long in the past and have endan-
gered the solvency of some producers, there are other sectors
where prices have gone up too easily, and there must be room
for change. With increasing price leadership and concentration
on the one hand, and productive units starved of capital on the
other, the price-fixing forces may be gaining ground. Justice
needs not only to be done but also to seem to be done, and
prices and incomes will both call for scrutiny.

If we are to have an understanding about wages and prices,
this presumes the extension of such contacts and co-operation as
exists at present. On the one hand, there must be some arrangement, perhaps informal but sufficiently effective to set a standard
in the light of which overall wage agreements are arrived at. On
the other, this can only be secured if price rises are kept within
justifiable maxima, whether by stimulating competition or by
more direct action. One cannot rule out, should it be necessary,
even an element of subsidisation of necessities, should the price
of necessities become part of an effective overall deal. The pricing
policy of nationally operated industries and services could prove
a sensitive point; it may have to be moderated so that they are

no longer called on to supply out of income as large a proportion as now of the costs of new capital expenditure: some price rises can be very disturbing when they are directly associated with government. There are bound to be problems of excessive pricing in the private sector also. Over and above this, a conscious policy for growth, in fact taking the form of the provision as a matter of national policy of new opportunities for employment by direct state action, is another possibility.

Any arrangement on the lines envisaged requires three participants. In the first place one has to envisage a trade union movement sufficiently strong to enable it to negotiate effectively and secure acceptance among its members of broad policies; second, industrial representation which also can make its views felt among those it represents; and lastly a government prepared to intervene to provide measures necessary for stimulating growth or for providing employment so that the policies agreed to by the unions can be justified to their members. This calls for a strengthening of bargaining power all round. In particular, the trade unions could be in a stronger position to take a lead and make their views felt among their followers if they were financially more secure. Lack of finance can make a trade union unwilling to take a leading and responsible position when it comes to industrial disputes, so that it leaves the field open to guerilla action. We have yet to see what the consequences of the Industrial Relations Act will be, and in particular whether its outcome will leave the unions in a stronger position to negotiate, so as to participate in wider understandings involving not only wages but prices and employment and growth. This assumes as an objective a common policy directed to economic expansion, and a climate and machinery in which local differences are dealt with responsibly and sensibly on both sides.

However, this aspect of the matter lies rather outside the limits of what is relevant to the present study. The short point is that without a policy – covering prices and incomes, employment and growth – which in practice emerges as being not unacceptable all round, any progress will labour under intolerable handicaps.

The second limitation concerns the extent to which particular types of policy can be used effectively. However desirable in general it may be to contain the level at which effective demand is increasing in order to keep down the rise in prices, one must take account of repercussions. Increases in indirect taxes which have the immediate direct effect of increasing prices, or cuts in social facilities which make additional demands on family expenditure, can only be expected to provoke demands for higher wages. There are points here relating both to scale and method. On scale, drastic action to give immediate results must risk being counter-productive, in any circumstances short of a national emergency approaching the threat of war. People cannot be expected to accept cuts in the standard of living as long as there is unemployment; they expect the unemployed to be put to work to produce more. A gradual reduction in the rate of growth of money incomes when that is getting out of hand is a different matter, and this brings in the question of method. The post-war credits scheme of the last war had much to recommend it in theory; in practice there was no slump at the end of the war, and no opportunity to release the post-war credits in order to counter depression, so that a useful device over the years became something of an irritant with arguments as to the circumstances in which they might be repaid to particular classes of holders. But in the future things could be otherwise, and one can conceive of circumstances in which some kind of compulsory loan (with clearly defined conditions as to when it could be released) could have a part to play as an alternative to an outright tax. At any rate it would not be as damaging as taxes directly raising prices, in order to reduce purchasing-power, in order to keep prices down.

Parallel with this there is the question of unemployment. No-one now admits to believing in industrial confrontation. Things were otherwise between the wars. In 1921 national income was £4·7 thousand million (at current prices); in 1922 it was £3·8 thousand million; it recovered somewhat but in 1932 it fell even lower and was £3·6 thousand million, and did not get back to the 1922 money level until 1937. Of course prices came down: retail prices were 25 per cent lower in 1932 than in 1922. But unemployment went up, from 14 per cent in 1922 (bad enough) to 22 per cent in 1932. The paralysing effects of unemployment and industrial confrontation on a national scale could be more devastating now.

These formidable statistics are recalled, not so much as a

warning of what might happen if industrial confrontation were allowed to develop, but as a reminder that for practical purposes there are strict limits as to the extent to which a policy leading to industrial action or to maintenance of unemployment dare be pushed. They are a further illustration of the general proposition that the conventional weapons to which we instinctively turn to deal with economic difficulties are limited in the uses to which they can be put. Used beyond a certain point, they become self-defeating: they give rise to countervailing action in the form of price increases or wage-demands which outweigh the purposes they were intended to achieve.

The third limitation is a financial one. It starts from the proposition that if we are to use reflationary measures – increasing money demand – as a method of stimulating a depressed economy and getting growth going, we need to pay special attention to the financing of productive industry.

One has to envisage as a first stage a money flow (tailored to help close a deflationary gap and to draw into active use available labour and resources) and to note its progress. The moment the wave reaches the counters of the retail distributors, the news is, as it were, telegraphed up the production chain in the form of orders whose impact effect is to call not only for a (continuing) higher rate of output but also for an immediate raising of the level in the productive pipeline at each stage back to the initial suppliers of materials. We can take it that from the outset money is being taken over the counter, and the flow of money will *in due course* reach the far end of the productive chain and then continue flowing. But there is a time interval and a readjustment to come in between. The orders are telegraphed forthwith, but even if immediate action is taken to put work in train, they will take time to complete and will involve outlays before they are delivered later and paid for later still. The public will be paying the retailer today for what he has sold from stock, but distributors, assemblers, component makers, material suppliers will all be called on to lay out money for what will be sold tomorrow and the day after, not only to meet the immediate increase, but to raise the level in the pipeline. The money taken over the counter will be banked some time before it is passed on in settlement, and will not be available – except in so far as the banker may pass it on in advances – to meet the need for finance further along the chain. This financial gap has to be bridged, and we have to assure ourselves of the adequacy of the financing flows both in total and in structure.

This difficulty, which is inherent in the situation, becomes more serious because of the observed fact that rising prices, while maintaining the level of personal saving, have been accompanied by a drain on industry's working capital. If we are to stimulate demand, we have to ensure that industry is in a position to expand output. If it fails to expand it, the rise in prices is accelerated; if output responds the rate of price increases falls. In the short run, even with labour and capacity available, a shortage of finance can restrict output, and adequate short run facilities will be needed to provide working capital. In the longer period finance is likely to be needed to provide the investment needed to increase capacity once expansion is under way. In either case, lack of finance which keeps down output leads to higher prices. We are directly concerned here not with the stimulation of demand, but the stimulation of supply which should go in parallel with growing demand.

It should be noted that we are faced in fact with three distinct problems of financing. They are: (i) transitional short-term finance which we have just been discussing; (ii) transitional medium and longer-term finance; (iii) permanent long-term finance. 'Transitional' under (i) means financial facilities required (in addition to bank and other regular finance) to achieve and maintain a higher level of output; 'transitional' under (ii) implies longer-term abnormal finance needed to make possible the further investment needed to maintain and continue the increasing level of output (over and above such regular finance as may be available) because of the changing levels of expectation on the part of borrowers and lenders in conditions of uncertainty (in particular over the outlook for prices); 'permanent' under (iii) raises issues of a different character, related to the question of how far normal financial facilities are satisfactory once an expanding economy is successfully in operation with the transitional problems overcome.

The following sections have something to say on each of these three financial problems.

2. *Transitional Short-term Finance*

What follows is concerned with the need for injecting short-term finance to enable production to expand in face of an induced expansion of demand.

The need for such a reinforcement arises from the spectacular depletion of the working capital of industry and commerce. As we have seen, since 1963 the net liquid assets of industrial and commercial companies have fallen by some £2,500 million between 1963 and 1970, an average fall of well over £300 million a year at a time when the purchasing power of the pound has been going down. In 1971 the position was much better. The banks and other institutions are now free and willing to lend, and in due course increased sales should lead to an increase in receipts and in profits and dividends. But banks must satisfy themselves as to the credit standing of their borrowers, and and it takes time for sales receipts to work through. In so far as industry is unable to keep pace with increasing demand because it cannot finance the necessary expansion in labour and materials, reflation leads to higher prices (and to further wage demands to compensate the rise in the cost of living). The case for injecting finance into the industrial sector at an early phase of increasing demand comes from the need to ensure expanded production from the beginning in order to prevent rises in prices.

We have to consider how much might be involved, its possible timing, where it might most be needed, and how it could be handled. In approaching these questions, the following points are relevant:

(i) While any calculations must take into account the value of physical increases of stocks and work in progress required, these by themselves are not a measure of the need for extra finance.

(ii) With the impetus coming from an effective increase in money demand at the outset, the financial requirement is not directly related to the demand, but rather to the time it takes to work back through the productive system. The buyer may pay cash for the finished product, but at the other end of the chain the producer has to lay out money for an increased supply in the pipeline for which he gets paid after an interval. The effect of this will be uneven; while in some cases there may be ample stocks, in others shortages may create bottlenecks impeding production.

(iii) In this there is an acceleration element involved. Thus if the purchaser increases his demand by 5 per cent and maintains it at this level, the supplier will find his stocks down from 100 to 95 and (unless he is carrying excess stocks) will need at least (a) a once and for all 5 per cent to restore his stock to the original level, and (b) a continuing 5 per cent more. Thus the supplier will need to put in an order to the distributor for 10 per cent or more, and the distributor in his turn will need to put in a larger order to the producer since he will also have to rebuild his stocks in addition to maintaining them at a continuous higher level. Thus there is a temporary phase (once and for all) when in addition to the assumed increase to meet the higher demand, some stock rebuilding has to be looked after. All this is, of course, a problem of bridging finance.

(iv) But it is an important problem because if the producer, faced with these increased demands, is short of money to increase his stocks of materials and components and his labour force, he will be under an inducement to increase prices to compensate himself for the output he cannot afford to expand.

(v) The remedy is quick and adequate once-for-all financing – which need not be particularly onerous – in order to avoid temporary bottlenecks which could delay the expansion process, and eliminate the danger that increased demand, meeting inelastic supplies, could give this further impetus to price increases.

(vi) On the other side of the account, we must bear in mind that the very increase in demand does generate a cash flow itself and that producers have already received tax concessions. We assume also that the banks continue to be free to lend to credit-worthy borrowers. But the scale on which they would be prepared to lend to individual borrowers could be limited by the depleted resources of the latter, since lack of internal finance will affect borrowing power externally. This points to a quick and effective injection of money as a prelude to a period of self-sustaining expansion.

How much would we need to inject by way of once-for-all short-term finance to support say a 5 per cent increase in output? What follows is admittedly speculative figuring, but once should be able to get some idea of the order of magnitude if we can find a figure consistent with (a) stopping, or substantially slowing down, the rate of deterioration in the liquid asset position of companies; (b) matching the jump in stocks in real terms which took place on the two previous occasions when G.D.P. increased by 5 per cent over the previous year; and (c) restoring the balance in the composition of the stock figures (a matter to be explained below). These are not to be added together; they are an attempt to look towards a distant object from three different directions.

(a) *Holding the liquid asset deterioration.* (What follows assumes that there is no further escalation in wage and price increases, and indeed that the rate of increase is moderating somewhat.) In 1969 the fall in liquid assets – by now a euphemism for increase in liquid liabilities, mainly bank borrowings – was some £700 million; in 1970 it was about the same. If, as an arbitrary exercise, we assume a 'next year' with 5 per cent increased demand following on the reflationary measures leading to an increased cash flow and freedom of bank lending together looking after the inevitable increase in additional stock requirements, and then ask how much would be needed to maintain liquid assets so that they do not deteriorate further, could one do much more than pick a round number from the air, and suggest £500 million? It could be more – but surely on any assumption of improvement as a result of expansion and greater profitability this would be unduly pessimistic. It could be less – but the apparent improvement in 1971 was in a year when production barely increased. So provisionally we note the figure of £500 million.

(b) *Matching previous increases.* The peak increase in domestic products and in stocks came in 1960 and 1964.

If we imagine the peak figure pattern repeating itself in a hypothetical next year, in '1973' the four sets of figures could be rounded at current prices to £40,000 million, £2,000 million, £1,000 million and 5·0 per cent plus.

Peak Year Increases in Stocks and Production
(At 1963 prices, G.D.P. figures at factor cost)

	G.D.P. (£ million)	G.D.P. increase on previous year (£ million)	Physical increase in stocks (£ million)	G.D.P. increase on previous year (%)
1960	24,639	1,148	628	4·9
1964	28,259	1,466	628	5·5

(Source: *National Income and Expenditure, 1971*)

To evaluate what £1,000 million increase in stocks over an expanding year might need in injected finance, we must make an assumption about the turnover period of stocks. Restricting the calculation to manufacturing industry, we can take an average period of two-thirds of a year. (Manufacturing output in 1964 £10,084 million; book value of stocks £6,910 million. Corresponding figures in 1969 £13,346 and £9,083). We can therefore reduce the £1,000 million to less than two-thirds since the financing problem is less acute outside the manufacturing field; in practice on this line of reasoning it is difficult to put the financial figure at much higher than £500 million, given the parallel relaxations in bank lending, etc.

We now have two guesses which pluck a figure of £500 million independently as being the sort of amount one might have to find if one were to make sure that finance is adequate to prevent hold-ups on the supply side arising from shortage of working capital.

(c) *Restoring balance in stocks.* This seeks to obtain a cross-check by a rather more detailed examination of some of the constitutents of the stock items. It is confined to manufacturing industry, which is the point where any serious hold-ups look most probable.

Over the same period G.D.P. increased by 15·2 per cent and manufacturing production by 16·9 per cent.

These figures are revealing. Industry has built up stocks some some of which could represent not planned reserves but accumulation of goods which have not moved quickly, and has economised on stocks of materials. Excess accumulations of finished goods do not present a problem when they turn into ready cash; shortages of materials must be a serious bottleneck. On this basis, there may be a short cut to an answer. Inject finance equivalent to twice the 1965–70 increase in materials and forget the rest. This would mean providing finance to the tune of £350 to £400 million (at 1971 prices) for the purchase of materials. If this could be done, and the rest of the system worked adequately, this might deal with the bottleneck problem, and in due course the need for bridging finance could disappear.

Manufacturing Industry: Composition of Stocks 1964–70

(£ million at 1963 prices)

	Materials and fuel	Work in progress	Finished goods	Total
End 1964	2,427	2,527	1,722	6,671
Inc. 1965–70	139	222	477	838
Inc. %	5·7%	8·8%	27·7%	12·6%

(Source: *National Income and Expenditure, 1971*; *Monthly Digest*)

To sum up the outcome of the three approaches: they are consistent with something of the order of £400 to £500 million being needed for extra working capital, mainly for the building up of stocks at an early phase of the expansion, if the output side were not to be held up.

How much weight is one to give to this sort of calculation? It must be confessed that there is a motive of provocation to some extent in the making of it; quite clearly it is – or ought to be – possible on the detailed information to make more serious guesses than this when the time comes, and if the present argument contributes to establishing the need for this, it will not have been time wasted.

One caveat should be entered. This argument is so far confined to a narrow problem relating to adequate working capital. It has not attempted to discuss whether there may not be reasons for more finance on medium term because (for example) the facilities for long-term finance start to break down on account of uncertainty over future interest rates. There may be other reasons also for a more generous transfusion. The purpose here is the limited one of raising the question of what one should do to avoid the risk of an increasing demand being met not by more production but by lengthening delivery dates and rising prices, and by imports.

Two wider questions still remain. The easier one is what answer should be given if anyone propounds the view that the argument so far developed is a fussing over trifles, and that an effective expansion of demand will be sufficiently forceful to stimulate the necessary output in one way or another – an argument in effect that it will all come right on the night. This is a tenable point of view, to which there are two answers. The first answer is simple: let us hope the critics are right. If all goes well, none of these actions need be taken, since things can be left to themselves. All that happens then is that some preparatory planning has proved unnecessary. But in the converse, action cannot be improvised and we cannot avoid the inflationary impetus. One makes the preparations, and if they are unnecessary we still have avoided the danger of being unprepared.

The other answer attempts to assess the probable position. At one extreme, if any increase in demand were moderate and gradual, and given no constraints on lending, the pressure on supply would be manageable and the dangers of lack of finance might not be serious. At the other extreme, if there were a sharp and discontinuous increase, the pressure grows more than in proportion as demand goes up. At the moment of writing (middle of 1972) the increase in effective demand has (disappointingly) still failed to make itself felt. There is little sign of expansion, and few complaints about shortage of finance. But the full effects of the March budget have yet to be felt. An increase in demand must come some time, and the longer it is delayed the sharper it may be, in which case bottlenecks, financial or otherwise, must be anticipated. The illustrative calculations made above assumed a 5 per cent jump in G.D.P., and suggest that the amount which might be used to good purpose and provide ready access to supporting bank finance could be of the order of £400–£500 million. All in all, this argument will have achieved its purpose if it has succeeded in drawing attention to the danger of an explosion in effective demand – possibly delayed – encountering an industrial output still suffering from the effects of past financial constraints. At any rate precautions are worth taking.

There is a second question which is harder to answer. The arguments and calculations so far put forward have been directed to the definition of a need and what it could cost to meet it. Nothing has been said about the problem of mechanics; of how the effective meeting of the need can be arranged and administered. A substantial facility of the kind proposed would encounter all kinds of claimants, many of whom were in need of money to pay off questionable liabilities or get themselves out of difficulties. There is a serious problem of selection. How can one ensure that the finance goes only to those who are in need of funds to finance production to meet increasing demand, and who given finance could look forward to a self-sustaining future?

There are several types of approach, which could be used separately or in combination. The simplest and most drastic: if the position is serious and the view is taken that some general stimulus to expansion on the supply side is urgently needed, much the best method might be a retrospective tax refund in respect of Corporation tax up to whatever total was felt to be appropriate. This would have the merit of adding unambiguously to internal finance and so strengthening borrowing power, of being once-for-all and of not involving any commitment to repeat it, since the tax rates would stay unchanged. (There would have to be an understanding that it was not distributed in dividends.)

No doubt there could be variations on this concept of a retrospective tax refund. In passing, such measures have the advantage, in comparison with announced prospective tax reductions, that their effect is immediate and that they need not be repeated.

In so far as the purpose of the relief is to stimulate the holdings of a greater volume of supplies, government facilities might perhaps be provided for the financing of purchases of specific materials, on attractive credit terms. Thus for an initial period (perhaps of one year?) the rate of interest could be nil or nominal, but after a point in time it goes up until it is considerably dearer than bank borrowing as long as the loan is not paid off. Such a facility could be provided for a limited period (to encourage people to make use of it) and then tapered off as the flow of additional spending comes in, bringing the necessary cash with it. It must be recognised that people will use this facility in part as a substitute for money they would have spent on their own account for materials. A much more serious difficulty is that any systematic and substantial plan for the organised purchase of raw materials could have the effect of driving up prices against the buyers and conceivably even precipitating a bout of competitive international buying, leading to pronounced if temporary price rises. A piecemeal building up of stocks in response to increased requirements could avoid such disruptive effects.

Finally there is a possibility of creating machinery by which applications for financial support come before some body which makes decisions in respect of them. The objection to this is that what we are concerned with is once-for-all action to get things moving, and temporary arrangements are difficult to improvise and to staff. The use of existing machinery could avoid this difficulty, but such machinery would have other functions to perform and conflicts of interest could arise.

To be effective, any loan finance of the kind envisaged could have to rank after bank borrowing: its purpose would be to strengthen the hand of the borrower so that his standing at his bank could be improved. Prior charges could only inhabit a prospective borrower's overall power to borrow.

3. *Transitional Medium-term and Longer-term Finance*

The need for finance discussed above arises from the drain on working capital which has left business ill equipped to expand output in face of any sharp increase in demand. The fear is that as demand goes up shortage of finance could inhibit the effective use of the available labour and resources, so that output could not keep pace and instead of a hoped-for increase in supply we get an increase in prices. The remedy suggested was in effect a piece of pump-priming; a once-for-all injection of finance to enable enterprises to carry the cost of an enlarged work force and a greater volume of material and components until the point came when the new income generated from expansion was able to sustain the enhanced volume of output. This could be looked on as a bridging operation, and is essentially concerned with working capital. In the short run the increment in working capital would be provided by this injection coupled with increased money from the banks; in the longer period accruing cash flow would make the position self-supporting. The word 'transitional' applies to an initial transition from a lower to a higher level of output.

The present section deals with a different need for finance, and with a different transition. Here the transition arises out of uncertainty about future interest rates, and the costs of finance in a world of changing price levels. Even if the generation of internal funds is at a satisfactory level, there remains the need for a regular supply of market finance. What is to be done if expectations in regard to prices and interest rates are impeding the supply of such longer-term finance?

The difficulty arises from a legacy and an obstacle. The legacy is that of an outstanding shortage of long-term capital because of past uncertainties and pressures: businesses have not been able to secure permanent finance freely on terms which they regard as acceptable. The result is financial improvisation, a need for funding or otherwise disposing of existing liabilities and an absence of accumulated resources to finance necessary permanent expansion. Funds are needed to tidy up existing liabilities and to enable undertakings to embark on further expansion. And here they are faced with an obstacle.

The obstacle arises from the fact that the calculation of money costs and rates of return is upset when it involves taking a view of prospective movements in the purchasing power of money. A rate of interest within sight of 10 per cent for gilt-edged (and irredeemables have gone nearly as high as that in the recent past) and more for industrial debentures is on the face of it a very high rate. But, as we have seen from the point of view of the lender it is unremunerative if prices are rising at 8 per cent per annum, and he has to pay tax on the proceeds on top of this. Rentiers, like wage-earners, look to maintaining their standard of living, and in real terms if prices are rising steeply they could fail to do so even when the returns on paper are as high as those quoted.

But with money rates of interest unchanged around the 10 per cent level, and no rise in prices, the return is very handsome, and now becomes a great burden on the borrower. The rate at which prices are rising must have a very powerful influence on the terms for lending and borrowing for any length of time ahead in the financial markets. A long-term rate of interest which is penury for the lender when prices are rising at 8 per cent per annum becomes usury when they are stable. And if interest rates are liable to fluctuate in response (among other things) to the rate of change in prices, how are borrowers to be expected to commit themselves for long periods into the future?

The borrowing enterprise has to make calculations about the profitability of its prospective operations, and then to see on what terms it can get the money; the investor has to make calculations as to what his income will be able to purchase if he is to commit himself for any long time ahead. With both parties having to allow for contingencies and unexpected developments, the area of possible agreement is much reduced. The result is a diminished volume of business on the long-term capital market, and an increased amount of short-term hand-to-mouth business, and a postponement of large-scale investment plans until the climate becomes more suitable. Steady long-term investment, both physical and financial, is a casualty of changing price-levels and in particular of price levels whose rate of change – and even direction – is liable to vary.

There are however several possibilities in handling this transition from a phase of uncertainty about future price levels to one of greater price stability. They include (a) Participation; (b) Convertible borrowing; (c) Covered short-term borrowing (that is, rolling forward short-term credits with supporting facilities); (d) Variable interest rates; and (e) Index-related borrowing; these are noted in turn.

(a) *Participation*. In its simple form this means equity finance: money raised on the basis of the sale of ordinary shares. This meets the difficulty in so far as the return to the investor becomes related to the success of the businesses. There are disadvantages: the investor cannot be sure of the return to expect, but this is partly compensated by the fact that if profits are larger than anticipated he can expect higher dividends. A more serious disadvantage was that money distributed by way of dividends is taxed twice over: while loan capital in the form of debentures or unsecured notes counts as an expense and is therefore paid out of companies earnings before the profits are taxed, ordinary dividends are paid out of profits after they have been charged for Corporation tax, and then the recipient is charged for the income tax. This was the

main obstacle to the increased use of equity finance,* and had
more or less killed the use of Preference shares: participating Preference Sharers, with for example an entitlement to a preferential
dividend supplemented by higher payments (up to a given maximum) if the equity received dividend above a certain rate, would
be a suitable method of dealing with an uncertain position by
relating the return to the performance of the company without
going the whole way in conceding participation in the business.

(b) *Convertible borrowing.* This deals with the problem by
providing an option to those lending on fixed interest to exchange
their holdings into ordinary shares on pre-arranged terms. One
method of doing this is to fix the terms of the exchange and the
particular points of time at which it can be exercised on each
given set of terms: i.e. you are entitled to transfer into ordinary
shares at such and such times only, and at a pre-arranged price
for each of the points during which you can exchange. This
involves a certain amount of complexity in fixing terms so as to
make them appear adequately attractive to the investor and fair
to both sides. This is a technical matter, and perhaps a more
serious difficulty is that it throws a series of decisions on to the
lender-investor, who in the usual way may be anxious to make
one decision only and leave it at that. Nevertheless, this seems a
reasonable way of dealing with the difficulty, on the assumption
that those providing the money are sufficiently informed to be
prepared to undertake the decision-making involved. In short,
such borrowing may appeal to institutions and professional investors, and deter the general public. This principle can – and has
been – extended to arrangements where the investor has at any
time the right free of charge to go to the borrowing company
and to transfer into Ordinary Shares at the middle market price
of the day.† This involves the company concerned in maintaining
a stock of unissued shares which it can use to meet the requests

---

* The difficulty is to be removed with the introduction of an imputation
system of corporation tax from April 1973. Companies that have had to
borrow disproportionately on prior charges can be expected to try to restore the balance by getting more equity into their capital structure once
the deterrent cost is off.

† See Gaston Défossé, *Les Obligations convertibles en actions*, Presses
Universitaires de France, 1970.

at any time. (In the case of the more common convertible the necessary provision is easier since the time for conversion and the price of conversion are both known.) From the point of view of the company, the existence of investors who have rights to change the shape of their investment with consequential repercussions on others with claims on the company could affect the company's ability to raise further capital. Those raising the finance will have to take such disadvantages into account.

(c) *Covered short-term borrowing.* Failing other expedients, the most obvious thing to do is to borrow on short-term, renewing the loan from period to period at whatever the going rate may be. The dangers of this are that the company may have difficulty in renewing if either its own fortunes or market conditions change for the worse. On either count it could have to face an obstacle if its short-term borrowings are at all substantial. One possible way around this is to arrange a facility for a long-term loan – an option as it were to borrow on terms the main conditions of which are specified though in part they may be dependent on market conditions of the day. One then pays a commitment fee to keep this option open. As long as this option is outstanding the company can borrow freely on short-term in the knowledge that it has for its continuing commitment fee acquired the services of a lender of last resort (or an underwriter, if one prefers to look at it in this way). Such a method has been used, but its feasibility is surely dependent on its being used rarely. If this were to spread widely, the cumulative risk being carried by the potential lenders of resort could become unrealistic, leaving the field open to financial innovators whose willingness to accept fees could exceed their capacity to float loans in an emergency. In such circumstances one would expect the intervention of the authorities. The thought remains, however, that the authorities themselves might in certain circumstances consider offering borrowing options against commitment fees, since they alone could be strong enough to carry this through on any scale. But such official last-resort underwriting could seem appropriate only for highly abnormal situations.

(d) *Variable interest rates.* Loans for a fixed period, with the rate of interest neither fixed nor dependent on the fortunes of the company, are well known. In practice changes in the rate of interest of the loan would follow changes in market rates. The problem here is that of defining the market rate to be chosen, but with an effectively functioning market there should be no inherent difficulty in this. (But there may be difficulties if things go wrong in the market, and the authorities have to intervene to impose a rate). This, then is an effective method, but only to the extent that the lender is satisfied to commit himself to follow the market into an unknown future until the loan matures.

(e) *Index-related borrowing*. The concept here is that of the rate of interest (and amount of repayments) in money terms being tied to movements in some agreed price index which represented change in the purchasing power of money. The concept is relatively simple, though the mechanics of the transition could be less so. But in this context the concept is peripheral to much wider issues. If medium-term borrowing arrangements are to be based on automatic purchasing power adjustments, why should not other arrangements – for example, wage agreements – be so based? Could it not be applied to long-term government borrowing? Once index arrangements becomes familiar, they could spread very rapidly, with far reaching consequences.

There are therefore these several methods which could be used to deal – singly or in combination – with the problems posed by the uncertainty arising from the possible discrepancy between real and money returns in conditions of changing prices. But it should be noted that none of them dissipate the uncertainty: their effect is to spread its incidence more fairly between borrower and lender.

And these methods have important institutional consequences. The fact that they have been tried – and tried successfully – is not conclusive. The question is whether they can be used effectively *on any scale* and in the existing institutional framework this is doubtful. Financial markets are largely dependent on exact assessments of narrow margins. Over a large part of the field institutions – banks and others – raise money on the basis of one rate of interest and pass it on at a marginally higher rate. Market pressures – the fact that competing institutions are doing exactly the same – provide a limit to the size of the margin. To quote a price for finance involves forming a view as to what it will cost to obtain. Escape clauses, or provisions for varying rates in accordance with some outside standard, whether it be the price level or rates in some different money market, do not eliminate uncertainty but pass its incidence back to the original lender, so making the lending less attractive in comparison with alternative outlets which may offer greater certainty. People buy ordinary shares traded on recognised stock markets where values are determined in the light of publicly available information, and spread their investment holiday over a range of securities to obtain diversification. But it is a long way from this to seeing widespread acceptance of securities with novel provisions in respect of which individual investors have to determine whether the prospects of gain outweigh the chances of loss.

In short, one cannot look to the ordinary private investor, whether he buys ordinary shares through his broker or through the medium of Unit Trusts, being a substantial purchaser of such securities. We are driven back on the institutions. Banks – at any rate U.K. deposit banks – are in the main concerned with short-term lending and do not deal in equity interests; they look for fixed returns. Unit Trusts are for the most part concerned with marketable securities which they can list in a prospectus. Insurance companies have more room for manoeuvre, but the extent to which they are prepared to involve themselves would be limited. Merchant banks have the experience which would enable them to deal with the sorts of problem involved, but their main concern is to support companies which are approaching the stage at which they can put forward a prospective public issue for underwriting, and that is a different matter.

In fact we are approaching the problem of industrial banking: that of specialised institutions providing finance on tailor-made conditions for areas of enterprise of which they have expert knowledge. It is well known that in the United Kingdom we have few such institutions, and those that have come into being have usually been in response to a particular need once it has become visible and pressing. For the rest, there is a tacit assumption that investment outlets involving complicated technology can still be handled on the basis of personal acquaintance and accounting principles. If past profits and prospective cash flows seem adequate, the business can be done provided the chaps are right; one must try to avoid getting too much involved with technical matters.

The question to which this section is directed is that of the provision of medium (and longer) term finance during the transition from a state of affairs in which prices are rising sharply to one where at any rate an approximate price stability gives some prospect of being attained. It is concerned with acute difficulties which can arise in a particular set of circumstances. But it is only a part of the wider problem of the adequacy of the machinery for long-term financing, and is best pursued further in the wider context.

There is however one technical point which might approximately be mentioned at this stage. It has emerged that a greater use of medium-term lending and borrowing could be helpful to industry in conditions of uncertainty. The market in medium-term securities is said still to be hampered by the stamp duty on transfers, although some improvement has been made. There might be scope for a further useful concession here.

4. *Permanent Long-term Finance*

So far we have identified two interim requirements for finance: on the one hand, that needed to increase output to keep pace with a sharp increase in stimulated demand, in so far as bank facilities by themselves may be inadequate; on the other, that needed to supply rather longer-term finance, when expectations of change in money rates and price levels are an obstacle, both to those seeking capital and to the borrowers/investors who would provide it. But these identified requirements lead to the more general problem of the regular provision of long-term finance, in particular for large-scale industrial units.

As has been observed, the traditional British financial-economic structure operates on the basis of a clear-cut distinction between the management of enterprise and the provision of finance. Successful enterprises are those which can establish their right to whatever finance may be needed on the basis of their record; they go to their banks for finance for recurring transactions and for temporary facilities, and when the time has come for expansion (beyond that made possible by retained profits) they go to their merchant bank which will arrange for the organising and underwriting of a new issue to be subscribed by the public (which in this case includes insurance companies and pension funds and other intermediaries as well as private individuals on their own account). The method on the face of it is clean and simple: a sensible division of labour on the asumption that those seeking funds have an achievement which can be examined and scrutinised publicly and which then gives access to a large market open to all suppliers of finance. But this rests on two presuppositions: that the greater part of enterprises in need of funds can be expected to reach a position of such strength that they can *openly* establish their claims to further finance at current rates, and that the exceptions which are unable to do so can be dealt with, temporarily or permanently, in other ways. Both of these implicit assumptions in their turn are in need of scrutiny.

To begin with, how far are those seeking new capital from the market in a position to put forward propositions based on past records and planned projections demonstrably so reasonable that they can be verified by accountants and financial editors on the basis of known information which is common property? Certainly many new issues – especially by the larger companies, but also by smaller companies which may have started to develop an attractive new line of business which appeals to the investor as an interesting speculation – are of this nature. Others, in the course of a period of economic difficulty, manifestly are not. They themselves may be, or they may be the heirs of, very distinguished companies, but the history of their immediate past may be disturbing and their future uncertain. What has gone wrong? How far have they got a self-sustaining existence ahead if they were put on their feet? How should this be done?

Rolls-Royce, Upper Clyde Shipbuilders, and other distinguished names come to mind. On the basis of common knowledge the informed member of the public – who reads, and is assumed to have to decide how money should be invested – is completely in the dark as to the real position, and inevitably so. The relevant questions are first, what went wrong, and second (and more important) was there a better course which could have been followed. This latter question is the one which matters; if the company were being overwhelmed by events over which it had no control, it is fruitless to dispute about which of the pathetic (and useless) alternatives was to be preferred to which. So we need to know if there was a course of action which could have brought good results, and beyond that whether this opportunity still exists. And so to the more forward-looking question, how far is there a sustainable future for the company in question, and on what scale of operation and in which direction?

Be it noted that these questions go vastly beyond ordinary accounting considerations of profit records and cash flows: they are right in the middle of technological and special market considerations, and even their assessment of costs requires the services of a whole range of experts over and above the accountants. Much of this is beyond the scope of the financial institution operating within conventional limits, and concerned to do its best for its clients. It may be a happy accident if the institution knows where to go for the appropriate technical advice; it cannot even be assumed to have this knowledge.

The sharp division between finance and industry does not obtain in the case of many other leading industrial countries. Historically in their case capital was not so plentiful, and financiers and managers had to work more closely together. But there are some examples of this combined approach in British history: not only in the great companies trading abroad, but above all in the case of mining groups operating overseas who have the responsibility both of securing the finance and of ensuring that highly complicated technical operations are carried through competently and successfully. The successful development of gold, diamonds and copper involved the provision and handling of finance in face of great technical complexities, and the ultimate outcome was the result of the fusing together of technical and financial expertise from the earliest stages. When money had to be solicited at arms length from strangers, the bulk of the work had already been done.

But what has been successfully applied in certain spheres of external investment has been applied to industry at home only by way of exception. To deal with specific problems, particular institutions have been created. In the depression between the wars, and under the influence of Montagu Norman and the Bank of England, the Bankers Industrial Development Company and the Securities Management Trust were set up to deal with the reorganisation of iron and steel and the cotton industry. After the last war, I.C.F.C. and F.C.I. were created to meet needs to which the Macmillian Committee had drawn attention.

The National Research and Development Corporation has been set up to develop and exploit new discoveries with the help of public funds, but taking an interest in the ultimate profits; it does combine technology and finance, with the emphasis on the former. More recently the Industrial Reorganisation Corporation played an active part in the industrial financing field, but I.R.C. has now been abolished. The frontier between finance and industry has its uncompromising guardians in the City still.

The argument here set out amounts to a statement of a need: for specialised financial institutions operating in defined areas and able both to provide finance on appropriate terms (which may not be orthodox terms) and to exercise responsibility on their own account for assessing technical situations as they arise, advising and if necessary reforming and replacing management, and even – in some circumstances – initiating and carrying through major restructuring within the industry with which they are concerned. They should operate on the basis of supporting and developing the long-term profitability of the industry, although if on national grounds it was thought desirable to give special support to an industry, they could administer the subsidy which the government decided to provide. They would be in a position to deal with an insolvent company on a commercial basis. That is to say, if they were providing, directly or as a channel, additional finance to refloat a company, they would be in a position to ensure that the money was used for reconstruction and development, and not to pay off existing creditors whose money had already been effectively lost. (In this way they would avoid the unhappy position in which an injection of government funds to support an embarrassed company is the start of a costly operation which has to cover not only the future, but to bail out in full existing creditors as well.) In so far as it was operating on its own funds it would be free to sell off companies it had refloated, could start new companies, and could acquire (at commercial prices) interests in existing companies if thought expedient. One of the advantages of a structure on such lines would mean that these institutions would be able to provide finance on equity terms, which is something that government departments are understandably unable or unwilling to do. Finally, the form of such new industrial financing agencies could with advantage be that of limited companies with adequate equity initially subscribed by the state. The question of whether they should be banks or not could be decided by experience, the test of a bank being whether they would be allowed to bid for deposits from the public.

The above sketch can only provide a starting-point for realistic discussion. The setting-up of the Industrial Development Executive in March 1972 promises more attention to these matters.

There is nothing new about such proposals. In 1909 a writer in *The Times* was arguing in favour of 'several industrial banks on continental lines, with a paid up capital of five to ten millions each'. (Translated into present values this would mean say £35 million to £70 million each.) At the end of the 1914/1918 war Professor Foxwell and the Committee on Financial Facilities were supporting this theme, urging German experience in its favour. In the early 1930s Professor Henry Clay was quoting American practice and was urging British banks to consider setting up subsidiary companies 'for the purpose of providing long-term capital'.* It is only in the 1960s that the banks have begun to move seriously in this direction, and even here the natural tendency has been to look more towards commerce than towards industry. The question of operating on a much larger and more systematic scale is still outstanding.

The case put so far has been on the basis of the necessity of combining the provision of finance with the necessary expert knowledge to see that appropriate use is made of it. The case can be reinforced on another ground: the need to provide a consistent flow of finance.

The very wide variations in the pattern of long-term financing can best be appreciated from a comparison of the returns to be got from investment in equities and in irredeemable gilt-edged.

The broad movements – going back to 1927 – may be summarised as follows:

(i) From 1927–29, from when the U.K. economy had re-

* These examples are taken from the present writer's *A Study of the Capital Market*, originally published in 1937, where the subject of industrial financing is dealt with at some length: see pages 201-231 and 275-290.

covered from the general strike up to the onset of depression, the long-term gilt-edged rate was of the order of $4\frac{1}{2}$ per cent; the running yield on ordinary shares was 1 or $1\frac{1}{2}$ per cent higher; the earnings yield was 4–$4\frac{1}{2}$ per cent higher still.

(ii) 1930–32: the years of depression, with sterling devalued in 1931. The gilt-edged rate started to fall in 1931 and continued to do so in 1932, when devaluation made the conversion of War Loan on to a $3\frac{1}{2}$ per cent basis possible. The dividend yield on shares went up to 8 per cent in 1931, and the earnings yield to over 13 per cent.

(iii) 1933–38: a cheap money period, with Bank rate at 2 per cent throughout. The gilt-edged rate was around 3·4 per cent at the beginning and end of the period, but had been below 3 per cent in 1935–36. For the most part ordinary shares gave a running yield of between $4\frac{1}{2}$ and $5\frac{1}{2}$ per cent. The earnings yield was considerably higher around 7 and 8 per cent for most of the period but moving upwards towards the end and reaching 10 per cent in 1938, with fears of war ahead.

Leaving out the war period and that of post war adjustments, one then notes:

(iv) 1950–55: gilts between $3\frac{1}{2}$ and $4\frac{1}{4}$ per cent (they have risen since the immediate post war funding operations) but ordinary shares yield for the most part between 2 and 3 per cent more, while earnings yields are very much higher. In 1952 the rates show the maximum spread.

(v) 1955–59: Rising tendencies in gilt-edged yields; stable tendencies in dividend running yields, falling slightly towards the end.

(vi) 1960–65: A startling reversal: In 1960 for the first time we have a reverse yield gap: long-term gilt rate has risen, the running yield has fallen, and one gets 0·61 per cent more on gilt-edged than on ordinary shares. However, if one looks at the earnings yield it is still higher than the gilt-edged rate. But the existence of the reverse yield gap continues.

(vii) 1966–71: In 1966 for the first time there is a reverse yield gap in favour of equity earnings compared with long-term gilts. By 1968 this had risen to over 3 per cent. This reflects a spectacular fall in the price of government irredeemable stocks between 1967 and 1969.

The following figures illustrate these developments.

Yields and Reverse Yields: Selected Years

| | Industrial Ordinary Shares | | Irredeemable gilt-edged | | |
	1 Dividend yield (%)	2 Earnings yield (%)	3 Yield (%)	Excess of 1 over 3	Excess of 2 over 3
1929	6·13	10·3	4·60	1·53	5·7
1931	8·03	13·3	4·39	3·64	8·9
1935	4·65	7·3	2·89	1·76	4·4
1952	7·16	22·1	4·23	2·93	17·8
1958	7·07	16·8	4·98	2·09	11·8
1960	4·81	10·8	5·42	−0·61	5·4
1966	5·08	6·85	7·01	−1·93	−0·16
1969	4·08	6·02	9·31	−5·23	−3·29
1971	3·83	5·92	9·2	−5·42	−3·33

Some may find the fuller figures of considerable interest; they will be found on pages 109 and 110.

This is not the place to try to disentangle the history of the relationship between safe fixed lending rates and the return on equity investments over the years. The contrasts and contradictions are the outcome (among other things) in part of the general movements of prices, in part of the efforts made to contain them, and in part the results of international movements of funds and of differences in interest rates to which this country, with its worldwide financial connections, has been particularly exposed.

But the line of argument which starts from the separation between financial and technical expertise is reinforced by this evidence of the swings in the returns on investment obtainable in the market, coupled with the certainty that what is happening in the price of outside finance required for industry is matched by variations in the volume in which it is available. We have to be prepared to find finance to ensure that in the long run the necessary rise in demand to increase employment is not frustrated by financial stringency restricting output. In the longer period we have to see that finance can be made available on suitable terms when increasing uncertainty as to what is happening to the price level is reflected in the public's ability to borrow and lend. Finally there is the need for a steady supply, not of subsidies, but of permanent finance coming forward at the pace at which it is needed. For these reasons also it is difficult to see how stability and progress can be achieved without substantial new developments in our financial organisation.

5. *Reversal points again: a Summary*

These are important, and perhaps there is one thing more to be said. To put matters into perspective, it is convenient to recall that particular lines of policy arrived at a point beyond which they first lose their effectiveness and then come to have a counter-productive effect. Among other, this applies to fiscal policy, credit policy, exchange rate policy and policy towards unemployment.

Fiscal policy. Increases in taxation and reductions in government expenditure taken by themselves must reduce money demand. This effect diminishes and then goes into reverse in so far as the taxes and the reductions in expenditure directly and visibly increase prices. At some point the cumulative effect of reductions in purchasing power will stimulate demands for higher pay which eventually become greater than the reduction in purchasing power which they are designed to achieve. It is a matter of calculation at what point fiscal policy becomes self-defeating. In this connection benefits subject to means test become significant. Thus in the case of the lower-paid a modest increase in pay (for example, to offset a rise in the cost of living) may take the recipient into an income bracket where he loses his concessions, possibly pays increased taxes as well, and finds that he is left with little of his pay rise. Large pay demands could be set off in this way.

Credit policy. The main purpose of a tight credit policy is to restrain consumption, in particular when purchasers may be attempting to anticipate a rise in prices. The danger is that, in spite of compensating incentives and concessions, it may have much more effect in restraining production, with especially unfortunate effects at times when increased output is needed to keep down prices. This aspect need not be elaborated again.

Exchange rate policy. Exchange depreciation in conditions of fully employed resources implies in the first instance a withdrawal of goods available for the domestic market and its diversion to foreign markets. This may improve the balance of payments (though it cannot be counted as inevitable that it should do so) but in the domestic market it acts in the direction of higher prices or a lower standard of living or a combination of the two. If there are resources, in terms of labour or industrial capacity, which are not being fully utilised, an export-led boom could be beneficial; otherwise there is the danger of a serious stimulus to inflation.

Policy towards unemployment. If unemployment is unequally spread, people can move from areas where work is scarce to areas where there is a demand for labour. (This applies especially to newcomers to the labour market.) Where there is general unemployment – as was the case between the wars – the opportunity to search for work disappears if over the whole country there are people already available for any work that is going in their particular locality. We do not use – or at any rate do not admit to using – unemployment as a weapon against inflation, but we must be on our guard against any spread in unemployment which made it general and inhibited movement in search of work.

To these may be added *Level of wage increases.* Where their average is less than the average of productivity increases, they can be accommodated without forcing a rise in the price level. Beyond this, with wages exceeding productivity, the way is thrown open to an open-ended upward movement with prices chasing wages and wages prices.

It should be noted that in all these five cases the reversal points are identifiable: the point at which demands for higher pay are stimulated in excess of possible reductions of spending power; the point at which tighter credit constricts output more than it can reduce spending; the point at which exchange depreciation reduces domestic supplies more than it stimulates output; the point at which the displacement of labour cannot lead to an effective reallocation of resources because further alternative employments will not be open; the point at which the rate of wage increases exceeds the rate at which output can be increased. Beyond these reversal points, stabilising forces become destabilising.

Why is it that these points seem to have been under-rated, so that we can almost detect an element of 'the dog that failed to bark in the night'? Is there a strain in our thinking that makes us feel that once the direction is right, we should go ahead undeterred by possible side-effects? There is always the double decision: first, is the course appropriate, and second up to what point should it be pursued. Perhaps it is fanciful to see in this a reluctance to accept the latter burden of added decision-making, and a somewhat metaphysical belief in appropriate economic modes of behaviour which – once discovered – can be left to work themselves out to a happy ending. So it may not be out of place to reaffirm a preference for pedestrian assessments made in the cold light of day.

ANNEX

Yields and Reverse Yields: 1927–1938, 1946–1971

| | Industrial Ordinary Shares | | Irredeemable gilt-edged | | |
	1 Dividend yield (%)	*2* Earnings yield (%)	*3* Yield (%)	*Excess of 1 over 3*	*Excess of 2 over 3*
1927	6·12	10·8	4·56	1·56	6·2
1928	5·60	10·2	4·47	1·13	5·7
1929	6·13	10·3	4·60	1·53	5·7
1930	7·26	12·1	4·48	2·78	7·6
1931	8·03	13·3	4·39	3·64	8·9
1932	6·99	10·6	3·74	3·25	6·9
1933	5·27	8·0	3·39	1·88	4·6
1934	4·64	7·4	3·10	1·54	4·3
1935	4·65	7·3	2·89	1·76	4·4
1936	4·50	7·3	2·93	1·57	4·4
1937	5·10	8·4	3·28	1·82	5·1
1938	5·19	10·0	3·38	1·81	6·6

Yields and Reverse Yields: 1927–1938, 1946–1971—contd.

	Industrial Ordinary Shares		Irredeemable gilt-edged		
	1 *Dividend* *yield* (%)	*2* *Earnings* *yield* (%)	*3* *Yield* (%)	*Excess* *of* *1 over 3*	*Excess* *of* *2 over 3*
1946	4·03	7·8	2·60	1·43	5·2
1947	4·57	9·1	2·76	1·71	6·3
1948	5·16	11·5	3·21	1·95	8·3
1949	5·66	14·9	3·30	2·36	11·6
1950	5·85	16·3	3·54	2·31	12·8
1951	5·61	16·6	3·78	1·83	12·8
1952	7·16	22·1	4·23	2·93	17·8
1953	6·92	17·9	4·08	2·84	13·8
1954	6·19	15·2	3·75	2·44	11·4
1955	6·17	16·5	4·17	2·00	12·3
1956	7·00	18·9	4·73	2·27	14·2
1957	6·91	17·2	4·98	1·93	12·2
1958	7·07	16·8	4·98	2·09	11·8
1959	5·27	11·4	4·82	0·45	6·6
1960	4·81	10·8	5·42	−0·61	5·4
1961	5·24	11·1	6·20	−0·86	4·9
1962	5·70	11·1	5·98	−0·28	5·1
1963	4·93	8·9	5·58	−0·65	3·3
	4·51	8·0	5·54	−1·03	2·46
1964	4·61	8·08	6·23	−1·62	1·85
1965	5·91	10·75	6·79	−0·88	3·96
1966	5·08	6·85	7·01	−1·93	−0·16
1967	5·13	6·85	6·87	−1·74	−0·02
1968	3·55	4·73	7·78	−4·23	−3·05
1969	4·08	6·02	9·31	−5·23	−3·29
1970	4·84	7·32	9·48	−4·64	−2·16
1971	3·83	5·92	9·25	−5·42	−3·33

(Sources: 1928–63, London and Cambridge Economic Service, *The British Economy: Key Statistics 1900–1970*. Table M. Gilt-edged represented by 2½% Consols. Figures averaged over the year. 1963–71, Bank of England, *Statistical Abstract, 1970* and *Quarterly Bulletin*. Gilt-edged represented by 3½% War Loan. Figures are end-June figures for each year.)

CHAPTER FIVE

Finance as a Constraint in a Developed Economy

1. *Scope*

What follows is an attempt to bring together the underlying issues, and to show their relevance to each other, and the general implications which emerge. In particular it is concerned with effective demand in a developed economy which is continuing to grow richer, and with the power of fiscal and credit measures to regulate it. It deals with these and other forces whose inter-action affects demand, output and prices. It examines the long-term significance of the continuing increase in real income and of increasing wealth per head.

The argument starts from the position that all assets (physical cash and active bank balances, other financial assets, physical assets) must be treated as part of a single assets structure since they are marginally interchangeable and alternatives from the point of view of those wishing to acquire them.

It attaches importance to the distinction between capacity to meet obligations *as they fall due* (liquidity) and capacity to meet them *ultimately* (net worth or net wealth), noting that the liquidity basis is the characteristic feature of current financial practice where transactions are so dovetailed that a failure to meet maturing payments can involve others in their turn if contingency margins are inadequate; it is through the provision of resort finance that control is made effective.

It introduces the concept of groups imposing (for example) price or wage increases through organised action. This is treated for purposes of analysis as equivalent to a tax, with implications (which may be conflicting) for prices and growth.

Under the heading of 'The Working Economy' it brings

together decision-making units, effective demand, liquidity and the assets structure; shows the impact of government and of other forces from outside the competitive market; and attempts to build up a picture of the way in which all these elements – with their interactions, repercussions and contradictions – operate to determine the price level.

Lastly the argument looks at some long-term implications of increasing wealth.

2. *Money and other Assets*

The argument to be developed here has as its foundation a broadly interpreted assets structure. In this money as such has no independent role to play. Cash and active bank balances are assets, along with loans and bonds and shares, dwellings and factories and plant. When one arranges assets in an approximate order of easy availability for transactions purposes, cash and bank deposits will come at the near end (with deposits in savings institutions close neighbours) and with land and physical assets in the distance towards the other end. There will also be a reverse order, with the least realisable assets probably offering the greater prospects of a profitable return, in compensation for the greater difficulty and expense of realising them. But either way money is in with the rest.

This is not just a matter of expository convenience. However distinctive the characteristics of the groups of assets, they have this in common, that there can be substitution and interchangeability between them. To attempt to draw a frontier between money and near-money is unrealistic; it is in movements across the area where the frontier would lie that significant developments are to be found. For a purpose such as this, money and other liquid assets (and likewise financial assets and physical assets) are alternatives, and outward disimilarities become irrelevant.

Such a view to many may be acceptable – as any rate as a working hypothesis – without further elaboration. At the same time the recrudescence of 'monetarist' views makes it desirable to examine more closely the limitations of the monetary concept.

In the first place, the concept is ambiguous. The Bank of England, faced with the problem of providing a total, publishes three alternative sets of figures of what is described as the 'money stock' of U.K. residents. They cover:

M1: Cash in hands of public, and private sector sterling current accounts with all banks.

M2: M1 total plus sterling time deposits with deposit banks and with discount houses.

M3: M2 total plus non-sterling accounts with all banks, sterling time deposits with 'other' banks, and public sector deposits with all banks.

These three estimates have an increasing coverage; they also, as it turns out, have different rates of growth. But the dividing line between 'other banks' and non-banks is arbitrary. All three versions exclude Building Societies and the Post Office and Trustee Savings banks, which in practice are bankers for large sections of the population. (The statistical effect of the inclusion could be massive.)*

There is no clear dividing line: in practice a bank is an institution which is recognised as such by the Bank of England, and makes returns accordingly. (Recognition may also be needed for other purposes from the Inland Revenue and the Department of Trade and Industry.) But there are other institutions which borrow to re-lend at a profit. In so far as they are able within the law to accept funds (paying interest) and lend funds (receiving interest) the money they owe to their depositors would be part of the money supply if they were formally to be recognised as banks. Credit creation is not confined to recognised banks. 'It would seem that existing and potential bank depositors – be they corporate or individual – are increasingly finding their needs met outside their bank account.' This was Lord Cromer, then Governor of the Bank of England, speaking in 1963.† Since then the credit squeeze on the existing banking system has led to more new institutions to facilitate the lending and borrowing of money, some of them recognised as banks and others not.

The concept of the money supply is ambiguous when the way

* For the case for inclusion see David Kern, 'The Implications of D.C.E.' *National Westminster Bank Review*, November 1970.

† *Banker*, June 1963, page 384.

is open for an arbitrary choice of institutions and classes of liability
to be included with the result that, wherever you draw the frontier, those on the far side are deemed not to be part of the money
supply but to be speeding the velocity of circulation.

To the charge of ambiguity there is a second objection – one
of logic – to add: the concept is inconsistent. The Bank of England's three versions of what it describes as the 'money stock'
carry with it the implication that it is made up of what people
have in their possession in the form of physical cash plus amounts
standing to their credit on the books of banking institutions on
which they can draw at will by writing a cheque or by giving
instructions which will be honoured within a (known) short space
of time. This is not so. Private individuals may largely have
become persuaded that when they write a cheque they must have
a credit balance. Business knows otherwise. Industrial and commercial companies taken together owe to their bankers far more –
well over £2,000 million more* – than they have standing to
their credit, and when they draw heavily on their overdrafts at
the same time they are likely to be adding to the stock of money
and not subtracting from it. This point troubled the Radcliffe
Committee, who enquired† what proportion of outstanding overdraft facilities were likely to be in use at any one time. The banking witnesses thought about 60 per cent, but added that of their
nature overdraft facilities could never be used to the full at one
and the same time: they were largely given for specific purposes,
and when the grain merchant paid the farmer, his increased
overdraft paid off that of the farmer, and so on down the line.
Nevertheless there is an element in unused borrowing facilities
which logically could be a part of the money stock if one wants to
be consistent; the trouble is that it is not logically quantifiable in
respect of any one point of time. The money stock is not like a
warehouse full of Dutch cheeses.

If our difficulty is that by taking no account of overdraft facilities we exclude unused spending power from our money figures,
in other countries there is an opposite difficulty. In the United
States overdrafts are rare, but it is quite common for account

* At the end of June 1971, companies had deposits of £3,519 million
and outstanding advances of £6,212 million. (*Bank of England Quarterly*).

† Evidence, Qs. 3625–3629.

holders to be expected to hold minimum balances on which they cannot draw and on which they get no interest ('compensating' balances). This can be a reasonable way of meeting bank charges – but it intrudes in calculations of the money stock. In countries where inflation is extremely heavy and where a usury law puts a relatively low ceiling on interest charges, matters can be happily adjusted by the granting of a loan of four times the amount required, three quarters of it to be kept as a minimum balance (earning no interest) in the account.*

Such special considerations apart, it is a matter of book-keeping choice how far *prospective* commitments are reflected in a particular account. A lending banker can say: 'Go ahead with the business; if it goes through, I will lend you the money' on such and such terms. Or he may say: 'You can take the money now, and repay it if the business falls through.' In the former case there is no entry in the books, or increase in the money supply. In the latter, the money supply is increased in respect of a loan as yet not in use. (All this apart from the extreme case of book entries not intended for use). The point is that it is not what is in the account alone which matters, but how far you have access to facilities if you need them. The state of an individual account at a given point of time does not show this.

How much weight are we to attach to these ambiguities and inconsistencies? One can concede at once that as long as we can fairly assume other things remaining equal (which may well be the case in the short run) it is obviously sensible to watch the totals of bank deposits. But having said this, one must face the reality that in most of the key situations other things are not unchanged. In conditions of stress, whether it be a financial crisis or an upsurge of prices, the money supply may be useful evidence if carefully interpreted, but that does not make it by itself a suitable guide to policy. Money is only one of a whole series of assets whose volumes and values depend on each other.

Ireland, with its experience of prolonged bank strikes, serves as a reminder and points a moral. When the banks are out, that side of the money supply is frozen. People add their own money supply, the rich known to be rich write cheques which in the

* M. H. Simonsen, 'The Problem of Interest Rates in Brazil', *BOLSA Review*, December 1967.

interim pass from hand to hand as currency. The sufferers are those whose financial standing is unknown or suspect. Eventually the banks reopen and the cheques are offset against each other; there may be some failures and a few acts of deliberate fraud where the cheques are not met by the end of the accounting. But the payments system by and large has continued to work, with the community creating its own money as it goes along.

The real difficulty lies in how we have come to think about money. We tend to regard it as something with a physical existence which can be counted and added up, which is demanded and supplied. But we have come a long way from gold coins in our pockets. What is money in the second half of the twentieth century?

Loosely, it is a unit of account. More exactly, it is an algebraical symbol – pound sterling (£), the dollar ($), the franc (F) – which provides a measure of indebtedness in each community in which the particular symbol is in use. If you have entered or are contemplating entering into a transaction, you know that you will have to pay £100 or will be due to receive $1,000 or whatever it may be, and that the Courts can be asked to enforce payment of the agreed figure. This may seem a pretty narrow definition, but the moment one gets beyond this one is involved in the problem of adjustment for price changes: money by itself is no longer an adequate standard of deferred payments, and even for accounting purposes there are complications – replacement cost as against original cost, and so on. We are left with money as a measure of indebtedness.

But what about money as a store of value? The store of value aspect is met by the assets structure as a whole; people do not want to hold either cash or non-interest bearing bank balances in excess of immediate requirements if there are more profitable outlets at their disposal provided they are not too far out of reach if the asset has to be realised.

Money as a means of payment? Payment is usually regarded as being made in cash or out of bank balances; basically it is made by book-keeping alterations in the structure of assets and liabilities. The relevant consideration is not just the amount of cash in an individual's possession, or the state of his bank account, but access to cash and to bank and other facilities. Any paying unit must have regard to the liquidity position arising from its assets structure: that is, its capacity to settle its obligations on the basis of its overall asset and liability position.

And so we are back at the starting point: we must begin by looking at the assets structure as a whole. This we now proceed to do.

3. The Assets Structure

In a community individuals and institutions have at their disposal physical assets (which on balance are accumulating) accompanied by an interlocking network of claims and obligations (which are continuously being extinguished, exchanged, transferred and added to).

Physical assets (leaving aside household possessions) fall under broad categories: agricultural and forest land, dwellings, other land and buildings, plant and equipment, stocks and work in progress. In the U.K. in 1966, the total value of all these physical assets was around £140 thousand million (and compares with a G.N.P. of some £33 thousand million).

Financial assets (balanced by equivalent liabilities, since what we are owed someone else owes) came to £190 thousand million, so every £1 of national physical assets was accompanied by an appreciably larger amount – 1.4, known as the 'financial interrelations ratio' – of financial claims/liabilities.* The broad categories would include: cash (including bank deposits), other deposits, loans, other debts, life insurance and pension provision, and company securities.

Assets are at the disposal of individuals (with a finite existence) and institutions (with a continuing one). Each spending unit will aim to have a mixture of assets which suits the particular circumstances. The individual – with a retirement ultimately in view – will be aiming to save to build up his insurance policies and pension fund contributions against the time when he will be giving up

* Figures from J. Revell and A. R. Roe, 'National Balance Sheets and National Accounting – a Progress Report', *Economic Trends*, May 1971. On the subject see also R. W. Goldsmith, *Financial Structure and Development;* and J. Revell, *The Wealth of the Nation.*

work. The business undertaking will be ploughing back profits in order to increase the income earning capacity of the business. The choice of assets will be dictated by particular requirements and by the special characteristics of the various assets. Some will be easily available for the purpose of making payments when needed, but may bring in a low return. Others, with a higher return and a prospect of capital appreciation, may not be easily realisable. The convenience of easy and certain availability may be balanced in other assets by better prospects of increased returns; those responsible for decision making will have to work out in what proportions they find it best to mix the various kinds of available asset. This includes physical as well as financial: the alternative to investing in shares or government bonds may be buying land or a house; the alternative to putting money into a savings bank may be to buy a new car. Assets vary in their characteristics, and have different attractions for different owners. Their respective prices will be adjusting themselves in accordance with supply and demand in changing circumstances; basically in adding to and changing the mix of assets the object of the holders will be to maximise wealth while at the same time maintaining their capability for meeting obligations.

What determines the choice between assets? Businesses add to plant machinery and stocks in the light of their prospects as seen by their managers. Individuals (houses apart) will be mainly concerned with financial assets. A wide range of considerations comes into play: chance of loss or gain, maturity, fixed or variable returns, marketability and cost of dealing, tax position of lenders, tax position of borrowers, convenience. One may note each of these in turn.

Chances of loss or gain. Companies may fail or become successes; they may raise or reduce their dividends. Debtors may default. In each case there is a risk of loss balanced by possibility of gain. The successful company increases its dividends and sees its share prices rise. Debtors may default, but if there is a danger of this, the rate of interest stipulated will be higher than it would otherwise have been. As long as payments continue, the higher return will be compensation for the risk. Over and above these special factors affecting the fortunes of particular borrowers, there may be a general risk of loss or chance of gain through movements of interest rates. There is also the distant but related question of movements in the general level of prices. If prices are tending to rise continuously, lenders on fixed terms face a diminishing purchasing power in respect of their income; the borrowers at the same time gain as their out-goings are less in real terms.

Maturity. Assume three types of interest rate depending on the length of time for which the loan is made: short-term rates (say under six months); medium-term rate (say therefrom and up to five years); and long-term (over five years). A lender has the advantage that he can lend on short term and then have the choice either of re-lending or of going into longer term securities if he thinks the terms will be more remunerative. Conversely the borrower will wish to borrow on long term if he knows he will need the money for that length of time, unless he has reason to suppose that long term rates will fall, in which case he could prefer to wait. Thus we have borrowers and lenders with money which they wish to secure or provide for varying lengths of term because of their particular circumstances, but they will also have to take into account the rates that they can get or may be forced to pay if they wait. Differentials between rates affect the volume of finance provided and demanded in respect of each time period. With general uncertainty, when people are unwilling to commit themselves for fear of a bad bargain which continues for a long time, there will be a disposition to do business on a short- or medium-term basis even if long-term finance is ultimately in the interest of both borrower and lender. In stable conditions one would expect short term rates to be lower than long term, since the lender retains the option of investing later, while the borrower is in an exposed position when he knows he will be compelled to reborrow. So on long term operations the borrower is prepared to pay a premium under normal conditions to secure the money for the full period of time, while the lender exacts the premium as compensation for parting with his funds and being unable to reacquire them prematurely without loss because interest rates have changed or for other reasons. But there are other circumstances as well. Sometimes there may be an exceptional demand for the use of temporary funds, which would force short term rates up and cause postponement of long term borrowing because shortage of funds has made the terms unfavourable for the time being.

Fixed interest and participating securities. Investors in long term fixed interest securities have to take account of changes in rates of interest, and changes in the purchasing power of money. When interest rates on new borrowing go up, those who have committed their money at the earlier rates of interest suffer a capital loss; no one will take over investments at the original price if there is a higher return in new securities. In the converse case, if the rate of interest falls those who have tied up their money at a higher rate gain. The position of the borrower is in reverse: he is worse off if he has committed himself to paying out at the higher rate over the long period. The other factor to be taken into account is that of changes in the value of money. When prices are rising the lender on fixed interest finds the purchasing power of his income falling; the borrower for his part will find that it is easier for him to pay once his profits or money income are rising with higher prices. When prices start falling it is the lender who benefits and the borrower who loses. Accordingly with uncertain prices one expects to find more investment in equity form, where remuneration follows the profitability of the business. Further, various compromise solutions have been worked out; fixed interest securities which have a provision enabling the holder at specific times to convert into equities at a prearranged price, or again types of security where the rate of interest can be varied in the light of movements of other interest rates, or in other ways. With such arrangements the conflict of interest between borrower and lender is made less acute.

Marketing and costs. Deposits in most institutions are easily withdrawable. Many stock exchange securities are widely dealt in, and these can be bought or sold immediately. Unit trusts cater for the small investor. Financial assets in general can be more easily turned into cash than physical assets; it may take considerable time to dispose of a house or property or a valuable painting. Even if there is no difficulty about buying or selling, the cost of doing so may vary considerably. To put money into a building society or a bank or into government savings facilities costs nothing. In dealing in stocks and shares there are not only commissions and charges, but there is a gap between buying and selling prices. The cost of investing is a material consideration, particularly in the case of the smaller investor who will want to avoid switching investments and incurring dealing charges.

Tax position of lenders. Lenders are subject to income tax and surtax, and to capital gains tax unless they (or the investments) are exempt. Savings certificates are not subject to any tax whatsoever, but the holding is limited. The money can be withdrawn readily, but there is some reduction of interest if the certificate is not held to maturity. Similar considerations apply to the Pay As You Earn scheme, where amounts are set aside monthly over a period of time and finally a substantial amount of interest is credited; here again there is no tax, but interest is foregone if there is a premature withdrawal. Building societies pay out free of income tax on the money invested with them, but surtax (if any) is payable by the recipients in full. There is no capital gains tax on U.K. government securities if held for a year. Nor is there such a tax on the sale of an owner-occupied house, though this would not apply to a second house if the owner had more than one.

Tax position of borrowers. When a business borrows on unsecured loans or on debentures this counts as a cost. Payments come out of untaxed profits, and this reduces the effective rate of interest substantially. This is no advantage however to a business making losses, if it has not got profits on which it is liable for tax.

Convenience. Deposits on current account in banks earn nothing in the way of interest. But the banks give facilities for making payments (through cheque books, credit cards and so on) and give help in various ways in looking after the financial affairs of their customers. These services, together with the possibility of borrowing, make it worth while for customers to maintain bank accounts.

This picture of the assets structure needs amplifying in two respects, it treats the structure as if it were more or less static, when in fact it is subject to constant change, and it neglects the reality that the assets structure is composed not only of assets in the sense of our physical possessions and financial claims, but also of financial liabilities – the claims which others have on us. It is not enough to net the two sides, and dispose of liabilities by subtraction from assets: the two exist side by side; one can add to assets while at the same time adding to liabilities; the relationship between assets and liabilities determine liquidity which in its term has profound effects on the speed and scale of the process of accumulation.

The assets structure is constantly changing because (a) obligations – i.e. claims/obligations, depending on which side you are on – are being settled; (b) obligations are being created; (c) obligations are being transferred or exchanged; (d) physical assets are being transferred or exchanged; (e) physical assets are being created.

Obligations are being settled. Only in some cases are both sides of a transaction settled simultaneously, in cash over the counter. More often there is a time lag. We receive our earnings at intervals; weekly or monthly or whatever it may be. But in the interval we have been working piling up a credit with our employer (who has an increasing debit towards us) which is settled on pay day. Similarly the outstanding liabilities from other transactions are in due course settled by a process of offsetting: the liabilities disappear, the common final stage being when cash passes or when the appropriate amount is transferred from one bank account to another.

Obligations are being created. This takes place when someone receives goods or services and agrees to pay for them later, whether in one payment or in a continuing series of payments as in leasing or renting.

Obligations are being transferred or exchanged. If we borrow from the banks, the bank takes over the obligation and settles it for us; in return we have an obligation to pay the bank. It should be noted that in the process the bank is bridging a time interval: at a later stage we expect to have claims maturing, so that when others meet their obligations to us we are able to repay the bank. But we can also transfer some existing continuing obligations – securities, or a lease – and in return receive a credit which we turn over to the bank.

Physical assets are being transferred and exchanged. Goods and services of all kinds are being transferred and exchanged, and over much of the field these transactions give rise to claims/ obligations falling due for subsequent settlement. In the narrower sense non-consumable physical assets are either wealth producing-machines, factories, stocks of components and materials – or objects which have value and give a continuing satisfaction.

Physical assets are being created. Production is continuing all the time, giving rise to claims on the business by those who work for it, claims by the business on those who acquired its products. But again treating physical assets in the narrower sense, the demand for machinery or buildings is rather more complicated a matter than that of consumer goods. What controls the level of demand for investment goods? There are of course large demands for replacement purposes, but over and above this the community is adding to its capital stock. We have to consider what determines the rate of this accumulation.

4. *The Accumulation Process*

The argument so far has put forward certain propositions. To begin with, it has been maintained that – leaving on one side money's specific purpose as a *measure* of indebtedness – its supposed uses as a store of value and as a means of payment can be discussed only in terms of the assets structure as a whole. (In the Keynesian terminology: the transactions motive, the precautionary motive and the speculative motive for holding money are to be interpreted more broadly as motives in selecting assets).* Next, an inspection of different kinds of assets has sought to show their contrasting and competing qualities; their very variety makes it inevitable that their relative attraction should change with individual circumstances and preferences. Further, since assets have in common the quality of being in some degree interchangeable,

---

* This is in line with Keynes' own thinking: see the *General Theory*, pages 357-8, where he speaks of Gesell as being 'unaware that money was not unique in having a liquidity-premium attached to it, but differed only in degree from many other articles, deriving its importance from having a greater liquidity-premium than any other article. Thus if currency notes were to be deprived of their liquidity-premium . . . a long series of substitutes would step into their shoes – bank-money, debts at call, foreign money, jewellery and the precious metals generally, and so forth.'

we should for the purpose of analysis consider them as a whole, treating as irrelevant any distinction between financial and physical assets. (This enables us to consider as part of a common process such acts of choice as that of a business undertaking balancing an increase in stocks of materials as against a stronger position at the bank; of a citizen deciding whether to borrow to buy his house, or to acquire unit trusts instead of replacing his car).

This takes us on to what to some may appear less inviting ground. It amounts to rejecting analysis on the basis of demand-and-supply of money taken by itself and moving in the direction of generalised demand-and-supply for assets. And indeed beyond it. Can we stop here? There is indeed no logical stopping place until we arrive at income and wealth being translated into consumption and accumulation. On this basis all transactions are interdependent, and to explain the process of change in the rate of accumulation of physical assets one must relate it to all other transactions. We are forced back to first principles as an alternative to partial explanations. We have to remind ourselves that any explanation must be consistent with a general framework; that we have our earning capacity, our expectations and our possessions, bound together by an instinct for self preservation, reinforced (in respect of those with appreciable possessions) by a developed sense of personal property. Given our capacities, our needs and our acquisitions, we seek to arrange the future.

From such a base, it is easier to see in perspective the motive forces which affect the ordering of assets and the scale of accumulation. It is a matter of choice tempered by arbitrage. Once we have provided for our consumption (or met with the outgoings of the business, as the case may be) we may be left with room to manoeuvre: we may have the choice of buying securities in one form or another, we may want to take the opportunity of paying off existing obligations, we may want to add physical possessions. Our room for manoeuvre in face of uncertainty is not necessarily circumscribed by the amount of unspent income we have at our disposal, since we may be in a position to borrow, and add to our assets more than we can immediately pay for, on the strength of future income or of immediate borrowing. The liquidity position will determine both our capacity to meet maturing obligations and in turn our capacity to enter into further obligations. This position will be determined not only by current and expected income, but also (to the extent that we have wealth in addition to earnings) by what we can make available by disposing of assets or by borrowing against them. Earned and unearned income, existing assets and capacity to borrow, all help to determine our ability to add to assets. This is the room for manoeuvre defined by the liquidity position which is the constraint on our ability to enlarge the asset structure.

What then decides the choice between adding to financial assets (balance with banks or savings institution, insurance policies, securities) and the accumulation of physical assets (houses and motor-cars in the case of individuals; plant, machinery and materials in the case of those in charge of a business)? We are choosing between the return we can get on the financial assets which most suit us on the one hand, and the return – whether by way of expenses saved or income received or otherwise – on the house purchase, or the additional investment made by the business. Note the 'or otherwise': at a time of rising prices it may be advantageous to buy early before prices go up. Note also that the choice will be affected not only by the return on the physical investment, but also by the return on the financial asset: a change in the attractiveness of the financial asset can stimulate or discourage the willingness to make physical investment as much as a change in the attractiveness of the latter itself. This holds good for business decisions as much as for personal decisions. The choice discussed here is a translation into real-world terms of the balance between the rate of interest obtainable on money and the marginal efficiency of capital obtainable on investment, in the Keynesian terminology. It attempts to substitute a more realistic and complicated assets structure for the theoretical concept of 'money'. In essence the argument is the same.

In two particular respects further elaboration is needed. There is the question of how liquidity works in acting as a constraint: that is, what determines capacity to pay. Then – following on from this – one has to see what external influences, as opposed to the bargains entered into by choice, come to bear on the value of assets.

5. *Liquidity and Spending Power*

As spending units – whether as individuals or business decision makers – we have to provide for our immediate needs before we can go on to make plans for future acquisitions balanced, as they are likely to be, by extended commitments. Our capacity for manoeuvre is circumscribed by the obligations, present and prospective, into which we have entered, and by our prospective receipts and existing assets. We have known outgoings, if we are to carry on with our current activities, and have earnings and income on which we can count. Beyond that, we have assets some of which may be easily realisable, and which we may be willing to realise in addition we have some access to borrowing facilities. These limits define our capacity to meet our obligations.

They also define the capacity to enter into further obligations. Decisions are again governed by prospective receipts and existing wealth and borrowing power on the one hand, and existing and prospective obligations on the other. In the light of these, and of a margin to meet the unforeseen, we determine the allocation of future spending, whether it be for consumption or for further acquisitions.

What happens if people fail to meet their obligations. In the last resort – as we know – individuals and companies can go bankrupt: such assets as they have are eventually realised and distributed amongst the creditors who, in so far as the amount available is inadequate, will ultimately be left with the loss. But this is the extreme case: in practice much can happen before this stage. When an individual defaults on obligations as they fall due, he may be able to sell property and personal possessions so that, losing some of his wealth and living more modestly he emerges the poorer, but still solvent. In the case of a business that runs out of working capital, rescue money may be brought in, or the business may be taken over, or in one way or another the original proprietors may have to dispose of a part of the business in return for necessary finance; and the business survives.

There are two quite distinct levels of failure. One of these is a failure of liquidity, where obligations entered into are not settled on time, but ultimately the creditors receive their money and the cost of mishaps or miscalculations is borne by the original spender or the original proprietors out of accumulated wealth. The other is failure outright; insolvency when after the assets have been realised there is not enough to pay all the creditors, and the creditors suffer for the difference. In effect there is a double standard; capacity to meet obligations *on due date* as they fall due, and capacity to meet obligations *ultimately.*

The former, the *liquidity* basis, is the foundation of our familiar business and financial arrangements, which are geared to the assumption that those who enter into current commitments must be in a position to meet them without having to postpone payment. For the individual it means having enough money coming in to meet the household expenses, day to day needs, and regular commitments, with enough in reserve to meet unexpected expenditures. For a business it is matching expected incomes and outgoings, having an adequate reserve of quick assets, and effective arrangements for extra finance which can be operated in case of need. The test of liquidity is the capacity to make payment on time, and it is on this basis that people are prepared to enter into current transactions. We fight shy of arrangements which could mean that we have to take people to court – and face delay – in order to extract payment by forcing them to dispose of a part of their wealth.

The other standard is the capacity to meet obligations ultimately: the test of *net wealth* (or net worth). In the case of the individual it is measured by what is left over after all obligations have been paid off – a hypothetical assumption. In the case of a company the corresponding calculation refers to what is left for the holders of the equity, the proprietors, after all other claimants have been disposed of. The net wealth test, in contrast to the liquidity test where prompt payment is assumed, allows for the possibility that payment may only take place after legal pressure, with all the associated unpleasantness, and assesses the prospects of recovery in full.

Professor W. T. Newlyn* using 'liquidity' in a wider sense which embraces both aspects, distinguishes three concepts:

Maturity: which appears to correspond to liquidity as used

* *Theory of Money* (1971 edition) pages 139-40.

here, measuring the relationship between maturing assets and liabilities.

Financial strength: the assessment of spending power 'assuming realisability of their financial assets and borrowing potential' by potential spenders. This seems to come close to the net wealth concept.

Easiness: 'the availability of money in relation to the level of transactions'.

The last concept is illuminating in that it draws attention to the fact that the quality of the realisability of assets depends not only on the conditions attaching to the contracts but also on the state of the market. In the case of the maturity/liquidity concept, a state of affairs which might be highly liquid when banks are lending freely, could well be tight when the banks clamp down. In the case of the financial strength/net wealth version, stock exchange or property market prices could directly affect the net wealth valuation; diminished 'easiness' could be subsidiary to this.*

The field which lies between liquidity and net wealth, to stick to our own terms, has considerable interest. The assumption that liquidity is a more restrictive standard than net wealth – a natural one in the circumstances – is by no means always true. Some businesses do get paid in advance: bookmakers, insurance companies, and traders offering goods by post through newspaper advertisements, for example. As long as business is increasing and the amount coming in covers what is going out, an accumulating loss may be effectively disguised. (Hence the special problem of the cut-price motor insurance firm.) Any business that is heading for disaster is likely to pass through a phase where it is somehow making ends meet on a day to day basis, though its overall net wealth is negative. (But its directors may be liable if they can be shown knowingly to have carried on with a business which is

* These comments assume that 'the availability of money' can in this context reasonably be treated as referring to financial facilities. Professor Newlyn holds that 'money is unique as the medium of exchange'. The present writer holds that money is only a measure of indebtedness, and that payments are made by rearrangement of claims: e.g. it is the cheque which is honoured, and not the bank balance, that makes the payment. But one would hope that this difference – whether it be a metaphysical divergence or a flat confrontation – need not deter agreement on the present point.

insolvent.) At the other extreme there are companies, owners of property or holders of oil or mineral concessions for example, who may be very short of cash but have immense potential wealth; they may also be potential targets for takeovers.

It is the field between liquidity and net wealth that credit facilities operate. Bankers, and other institutions which have funds available, are narrowing the gap between liquidity and net wealth when they make a loan which adds to liquid assets against the security of less liquid assets; that is how financing institutions make their profit. Conversely, when they reduce the scale of their lending, they increase the gap, thereby increasing financial pressure. The basic credit process can be explained in terms of the gap between liquidity and net wealth, and the possibility of increasing or reducing it.

It follows from this that there is scope, especially in conditions of squeeze, for financial institutions to develop new ways of making more of net wealth liquid. Negotiable certificates of deposit now enable a company to put money on deposit for a fixed period ahead at a correspondingly more favourable rate of interest, but nevertheless to turn it into cash at any time by passing it on to another holder, taking the relevant loss or profit resulting from any interest rate changes in the market in the interval. The bank thus retains the deposit for the full period; only the ownership of the deposit has changed.

Another device, described in an article by Edward Davis already referred to,* is that of sale and lease-back. A business sells its property outright, collecting cash, and rents it back on a lease. This provides a ready reinforcement of the cash position, though in the future there is the problem of renegotiating the lease when the time comes, should the company wish to continue in the same premises.

Finally, in the long term there is the question of how far it will be necessary or possible to maintain the distinction between the liquidity and net wealth standards in a world which is getting richer, and financial devices, including credit insurance, are becoming more sophisticated. But that is a speculation which will be developed later in a wider context.

* *Bankers' Magazine*, December 1970.

6. *Agreed and Imposed Obligations*

So far we have been concerned with arrangements voluntarily entered into by the parties concerned, whether for cash settlement, deferred payments, continuing payments or otherwise. Someone in return for a sale or service performed is to receive a payment or a series of payments. These are the claims/obligations which are constantly being settled, coming into being, continuing; everything from sales, and purchases, loans, leases, insurance to contracts of employment.

But there are other types of obligation to be considered; above all, those instituted by public authorities. The authorities can decide on obligations which they are prepared voluntarily to enter into. And they can impose obligations or forego claims unilaterally.

The first of these aspects is concerned with borrowing, debt management and credit policy and the price and type of securities they are prepared to offer in the course of managing their borrowing needs. National and local authorities are always engaged in making repayments and offering new securities and forms of savings. They can vary the terms. They can vary the maturities. This is taking place even though the total volume of official debt outstanding is unchanged: at any time they can change going rates or the associated conditions. They operate in the market and – subject to what the market is prepared to accept – can make different types of security more or less attractive. This is a generalised view of what can be more narrowly described as debt switching and open market operations.

The other line of action open to the authorities is more powerful; it is fiscal policy, and operates through changes in the total volume of borrowing brought about by changes in taxation and expenditure. When government increases its tax revenue it imposes obligations unilaterally: there comes into existence a claim under which the government is entitled to receive, and an obligation on tax payers to pay. When government reduces taxation it is relieving the taxpayer of some of his obligations. Both cases follow from a unilateral act, which has consequences for others.

It is important to note the distinction between the first type of official action – debt switching and open market operations – where the citizen is a voluntary participant, and the latter type, where governments and public bodies are empowered to make a levy on the public (or in the opposite case can unilaterally grant a relief). Here we have the essentials of financial management: control through the manipulation of credit terms and the availability of credit on the one hand; and more direct operation on the flow of effective demand through spending and fiscal measures on the other.

But it is not only governments who can impose obligations unilaterally. It is here argued that among the factors playing their part in directly determining effective demand we must also include the exercise of power to impose obligations unilaterally by organised groups, such as business, labour and (hypothetically at any rate) in the opposite direction, by consumers. Thus the value of assets will be determined not only by what may be agreed voluntarily between spending units, or between spending units and government in respect of government debts, but also by action taken by organised business, labour and (conceivably) consumers, in addition to government.

How do these additional forces operate?

First, organised business. In competitive conditions any business is free to undertake what another business is not prepared to do. In practice it can (in appropriate conditions) be advantageous for a business (or group of businesses) to decide to restrict output or to work on a system of minimum prices in such a way as to secure a higher aggregrate of profit than would have been the case under competitive conditions. This could become the equivalent of a tax imposed on the consumer, to the extent that he is forced to pay more than otherwise he need have done. Often there may be good reasons by such a policy is inexpedient, and the advantage is not pressed. There may be legal difficulties, or threats for potential rivals. But the possibility remains of organised business finding itself with the power to impose prices higher than are necessary. One can envisage circumstances in which this could have major effects.

Second, organised labour. The upward pressure for increased money wages increased spectacularly from the second half of 1969 onwards. It is often assumed that it is in the interest of organised business to resist wage demands; but business has the alternative possibility of making wage concessions and putting up prices. This may well become the preferred course if business feels itself in a weak position and competition is not strong, the inclination being to exploit existing customers rather than go out to fight for new markets.

Third, organised consumers. Consumers are interested in critical appreciation of what is offered to them, but so far there is nothing which can be described as 'organised' consumer activities in the sense of direct action: for example, consumer pressures taking the form of collective negotiations reinforced by the threat of boycott of particular suppliers who are thought to have offended. The explanation perhaps is that in the main consumers are faced with distributors and retailers who on the whole have maintained a high degree of competitiveness. Consumer pressure cannot be ruled out. But as yet it is not a defensive force seeking to keep down price rises.

That leaves the remaining defence against rising prices in the hands of organised government. Here we have government action on restrictive practices, voluntary or semi-voluntary action on prices and incomes, and action through the financial machine. The last is thought of as the main weapon available to the authorities, but it is subject to the disadvantage that in practice its power is limited; taxes – particularly indirect taxes – intended to reduce consumption demand in order to keep down prices can have the opposite effect of immediately accelerating rising prices, thereby increasing the pressure for higher incomes and in turn stimulating further price rises. Indeed, a vigorous use of fiscal and credit weapons beyond a certain point can be more effective in curtailing supply than in restraining demand.

The following pattern emerges. The flow of effective demand in money terms, and the flow of output that meets it, is not only determined by organised government (through its budgetary and credit policies) but also by organised groups in the community exercising their bargaining power. The bargaining power at their disposal will vary with circumstances. That of organised business may be weak when business is brisk and competition active; but it may become stronger if demand weakens, profits are low, finance scarce. The urge to get in first in new markets ceases; more concerns are content to follow price leaders; business mergers take place in self-defence; the inducement to expand disappears. Forces can gather to defend and maintain prices and to avoid expansionary commitments. In such circumstances business will provide neither a protection against price rises, nor inducement to growth. In so far as it is forced to pay higher wages, it will tend to reduce the numbers it employs. In course of time, organised business can consolidate – nationally and even internationally – around its common interest, defending the status quo and avoiding change and growth. The restrictive aspect of this policy could predominate, and act as an inflationary influence by keeping down supply and holding up growth.

The interest of organised labour is not in direct conflict with that of business. Labour's position may be (not unreasonably on the face of it) that if there is unemployment and unused capacity, what is needed is an increase in demand, and this is brought about by higher wages. The argument that higher wages will mean higher unemployment seems unimpressive; if there is to be higher unemployment because money wages go up, would there not have been at least as much such unemployment (or more) if money wages had not gone up? If nine-tenths of the work force produce as much as was done by the full number before, are not they entitled to an increase? If some are getting wage increases because they are fortunate enough to be in occupations where there is room for increasing productivity, should not others share the benefit? After all, with unutilised capacity and men out of work, what reason is there for going slow on wage demands – especially when there is a handsome surplus in the balance of payments. Indeed, ought there not to be room for some improvement in the standard of living?

From these positions, both business and labour press on parallel (one can barely resist writing 'complementary') courses which together force up prices: because (in the case of labour) excessive demands stimulate further excessive demands; because (in the case of business) shortage of finance leads to a rigorous pruning of expenses and stagnation in place of expansion, while it may prove cheaper (if you are short of funds) to agree wage demands, cut back employment, raise your selling price and hope for the best; because (in the case of both) the resulting confusion leads to loss of output.

So these two forces combine to throw us off course. What about forces in the opposite direction?

There is the hypothesis of organised consumers. One can toy with the prospect of a consumer movement adopting tactics of protest, boycott and organised intervention against industrial groupings which appear to be working against their interest, but it has not come about, does not yet look like coming about, and could be effective only on a limited scale.

Next, organised government. The effective of prolonged credit restriction appears to have been to hold back expansion even though industry has been faced by some increase in demand in money terms, and possibly to weaken seriously industry's capacity to bargain in face of exaggerated wage pressures. The effect of budgetary policy has tended to identify the increases of taxation and reduction of expenditure with increases in prices, because as applied that has often been their immediate visible effect, and this outweighs the hoped for indirect effect that the consequent reduction in consumption would in due course help to contain prices. It is true that since 1969 a spectacular turn-round in the balance of payments has been achieved, but this opens up the question whether a slower turn-round and a more modest application of the methods involved would not have led to more satisfactory results by minimising repercussions.

With the relaxations of 1971, one must hope that careful handling both of the reflation of demand and of the parallel strengthening of the financial position of business undertakings will succeed in avoiding the opposite dilemma, that of effective demand growing faster than production is able to increase supply in spite of available labour and capacity. If this is to be handled successfully, it means more than easing bank lending and reducing taxes on consumers and producers. An agreed prices and incomes policy worked with good will, and effective financing institutions capable of a discriminating injection of needed funds for producers, seem indispensable.

But much of this analysis of passing developments is as it were *obiter dicta*. The purpose of this stage of the argument is to bring asumptions into perspective. In particular, one must not assume that effective demand is controlled and controllable by financial (i.e. fiscal and monetary) action alone. The determinants of effective demand, and of the production which it effectively elicits on the supply side, include the bargaining power of labour and business. In part such bargaining leads to imposed and not just agreed obligations. The policy decisions of organised labour on wages, and or organised business on output and pricing, affect directly not only the price level but also the make-up of the assets structure with which we were earlier concerned. They influence the rate at which consumers and producers are prepared or enabled to enter into new obligations, or the prices at which such arrangements are made, in the same way as open-market operations or tax changes. The outcome of these conflicting forces will be to determine the cost of living, the rate of growth and (more remotely) such things as the volume of cash and the level of current bank deposits.

7. Working Economy

It remains to fit the pieces together.

To begin with, the main elements in a competitive economy: the decision-making units, effective money demand, the assets structure, and the liquidity position. Then the outside forces which are in a position to intervene and superimpose obligations on those which would otherwise be settled by the market.

The decision-making units. The economy is built up of spending units (personal and business) which are in receipt of income and have wealth at their disposal, and decide on the scale and direction of their current outlays. They balance up how much they propose to spend on current consumption on the one hand, and on the other how they will re-arrange their assets structure (having regard to the need for liquidity, future income, growth possibilities and satisfaction, in an appropriate mix). Each spending unit – whether person or undertaking – will be concerned to maintain and improve its position. The circumstances vary, whether for individual or business, but in general there will be an element of predictability in each case which when aggregated for the whole economy exposes a relatively clear-cut pattern. Thus it is possible to anticipate – effectively if not always exactly – how the choice and requirements will be spread: that is, we can tell what people will need to buy and how they will spend their money. Households have defined problems; businesses wish to continue and pursue their accepted goals. This element of pre-dictability is the basis on which a specialised economy operates; if choices were random and unpredetermined, this would remove the possibility of anticipating needs, and of planning production ahead of the demand it is to meet.

Effective money demand. By 'money' what is meant here is that the business is transacted in terms of claims and obligations labelled and calculated in money terms, not that such business is settled in physical cash or through one of the clearing banks. In practice payment may be made in cash or cheques, and it can also be deferred. Effectively, ignoring the mechanics, it is made by offsetting claims against obligations: passing on income or ceding assets, or assuming a future obligation. It is important to note that the wealthier the society, the less spending need be tied to income. Where the society is poor, or in the poorer reaches of an affluent society, the income position is a major constraint on expenditure. The wealthy society is in a freer position, since the rich can pledge or dispose of their possessions should they wish to supplement their income. The constraints are not the same, and the decisions can be more volatile.

The Liquidity Position. This is the constraint on spending. Every spending unit has income it expects to get in, continuing and/or expected obligations which it will have to meet, and con-tingencies for which it must be prepared to provide. The margin between prospective income and prospective outlay will in most cases be buttressed by some measure – greater or smaller – of reserve in the form of assets. But the margin may be tight. The room for manoeuvre is restricted further by the institutional arrangements governing finance. The effective limit is not that you must be able to pay, but that you must be able to *pay on time.* Default seriously on your payments, and your credit is damaged: assets of substantial value which are not available immediately may not save you from the serious disadvantages. This particular institutional convention is the foundation of current financial pratice, where transactions are so dovetailed that one failure may carry others in its turn, and consequential arrangements for emergency finance may be onerous. Accordingly the assets that people hold are carefully chosen to maintain adequate liquidity, so that enough can be realised without substantial loss if it is necessary to meet unforeseen financial demands. This emphasis on payment on due date, it must be stressed, is a convention; it does not follow that it is a necessary convention, and it is a matter for speculation as to what would happen in a rich country with wealth well spread. Would the payment constraint become much weaker, and would there be inflationary consequences?

Assets Structure. The asset structure of a spending unit consists of physical assets plus financial claims minus financial obligations. For the community as a whole financial claims and obligations are equal by definition, since what someone is owed someone else owes, but it is not so in the case of the individual units who may on balance be either debtors or creditors. When an asset holder has the choice of, for example, borrowing cheaply and lending at a profit he will (other circumstances being satisfactory) increase his liability in order to re-lend, so that the financial superstructure is expanded by a double set of transactions. The outcome is that A owes money to B while he has a claim on C to whom he has re-lent the money he borrowed from B. In the converse case, A may find it profitable to dispose of a claim in order to pay off a debt, reducing both sides of the financial superstructure. Much therefore turns on (a) the marketability/liquidity of particular assets, and (b) the relative price of assets, which in turn will be affected by the income they bring in. Hence the attempt to maintain a balanced assets structure, given the objective of combining adequate liquidity with an adequate return, and taking into account that the less realisable claims should bring in the higher return.

But what about physical assets, deliberately included alongside financial assets? In an expanding economy, by definition, the volume of physical assets is increasing after making due allowance for replacement. What determines the change in demand for physical assets? At any point of time the rate of accumulation of such assets will be determined by how far it pays to dispose of financial claims, or increase financial obligations, in order to acquire physical assets. The scale on which spending units can directly or indirectly finance accumulation will be circumscribed by capacity to settle obligations as they fall due having regards to income and assets, that is to the liquidity position, since capacity to settle obligations determines capacity to enter into them.

The summary up to this point has been subject to a limiting assumption; that all these matters are settled, as it were, on a market basis, by choice and by voluntary bargains within a competitive economy freely comparing alternatives. It remains to bring into the picture the element of an outside intervention, whether it comes from government or is imposed by organised groups.

How do the authorities intervene in this mechanism of choice – money demand – liquidity – assets? First, the authorities can move to influence assets structure by altering the relative prices of different assets through the weight of their own borrowing policy. By funding and unfunding, by varying the maturities and interest rates (and other conditions) they can affect relative prices and returns in the market. In the process they can change the liquidity position of asset holders and the relative attractions of assets on offer. This means a change both in people's capacity to add to their physical assets and their willingness to do so. Thus by tightening credit through debt policy and open market operations they can make it more difficult for business to borrow to expand. Second, they can affect liquidity more directly, by operating on the conventions and institutions which make up the liquidity frame-work; through reserve ratios, special reserve arrangements, limitations on borrowing or lending. Further, they can create special lending institutions, or discriminate against certain types of finance. Third, the authorities – and this is their most important weapon – can change the balance between taxing and spending; they can impose obligations unilaterally on the community by tax measures, withdrawing purchasing power, or they can remit taxes, thereby increasing it. (The purpose would be to increase or decrease effective demand, but there will be repercussions). Fourth, they can take measures which have specific effects on particular groups and sections of the community. Examples include development area policy, special taxes or special subsidies for particular industries, the creation of special institutions.

It will be noted that, with the exception of the first element, all the above are obligations imposed by government; they are not agreed or negotiated. (In the exception, the government offer loans etc., on given terms, and purchasers are free to refuse to deal). But it is not only government that can impose obligations: organised groups may be in a position to do the same. For purposes of this analysis successfully operated restrictive practices, whether price rises or wage settlements, can be treated as equivalent to a tax in so far as they raise prices higher than they otherwise would have been. The exactions so imposed can set in train a chain of events in the way that a tax will. Organised business and organised labour in practice may have power to impose obligations on the rest of the community which will be different from those which otherwise would have been arrived at by unimpeded bargaining.

This leads on to the matter of repercussions. The intentions of policies, and their consequences, can become inconsistent to the point of contradiction. The argument in favour of a tax on a commodity may be that prices are rising too fast and purchasing power should therefore be reduced. But the very imposition of the tax raises prices and thereby may provoke an increase in purchasing power (through wage claims) in excess of any possible benefit from the tax itself. A drastic turnround in the balance of payments may set off price rises (though the cut in available domestic supplies) which would have been avoided had the planned improvement been at half the rate. Economic policy making runs the danger of encountering negative returns.

So one comes up to the question: what determines the price level?

The formal answer is: effective money demand; the output elicited by it; interactions and repercussions between them. In spelling out the answer it will be convenient to follow this framework.

What determines effective demand? The aggregate of decisions (expressed in money terms) made by spending units. These will be governed by (a) the existing institutional financial framework; (b) the liquidity position of each spending unit, which will reflect current and expected income and outgoings and the degree to which accumulated wealth could be mobilised to reinforce desired

additions to consumption or to accumulation; and (c) expectations
as to the expediency of accelerating or delaying the rate of purchases.

Changes in effective demand are the outcome of changes in
(a), (b) and (c), which need not be in the same direction. Changes
in (a) will reflect decisions imposed by the monetary authorities
or adopted by market operators in respect of available financial
facilities. Changes in (b) will reflect changes in net official spending, coupled with agreed or imposed changes in money remuneration. The changes already mentioned – and in particular those
under (b) – can bring about changes in (c), expectations.

What determines output? The aggregate of decisions (assessed
in money terms) made by the managers of business undertakings.
These will be governed by (A) the productive resources and technical knowledge at their disposal; (B) availability of capacity and
labour; (C) adequate current finance to pay for labour and
materials up to a maximum level of profitability; (D) the level
at which wages and prices are fixed; (E) expectations as to the
expediency of increasing or reducing the rate of output. One
should also add (for the long run) (F) accumulation of physical
capital for the purpose of increasing production.

Changes in output are the outcome of changes in any or all
of these items. (A) and (B) impose absolute limits on the extent
to which physical output could be increased.

Interactions and repercussions are at the heart of the matter.
An increase in money demand with an unchanged physical output will start prices moving up. The same with a proportionate
increase in physical output through more employment could keep
prices stable. An increase in costs of output (D) arising from wage
concessions would mean (via demand (b), increased income) an
increase in prices except in so far as it is balanced by increased productivity. An increase in the price of output through a tax imposed
and passed on in price increases could have the repercussion of
a successful demand for increased income (demand (b)) which
would be reflected back as increased wage costs (output (D)) leading to a further increase in prices. Money demand pegged with
output costs increased could lead to lower output, lower employment, higher prices – but we know that there are likely to be
repercussions when anyone attempts to enforce the assumption of

money demand pegged. But one can go on playing this game endlessly.

One cannot point to any inherent tendency to stability in the price level. The nearest to a stabiliser that there may be lies in the unwillingness of any price maker to risk starting a change because of possible repercussions on his competitive position. There is reason to believe that this does operate to a considerable extent in favourable circumstances, but one cannot claim much more than that. Increasing productivity does, however, provide a narrow margin for manoeuvre. To the extent that increasing costs can be kept within the range of increasing productivity, prices need not rise. But this is a difficult formula within which to operate, since the average level of productivity increases is very much less than that of those sectors of industry which show the greatest productivity gains, and it is the latter which tend to set the pace. Once money wages are rising at a rate greater than average productivity, the price level is moving upwards with no inherent stabiliser to stop it.

8. *Implications*

It may be relevant to recall features of the analysis as set out in these pages.* To begin with, the role of money in itself was confined to that of an accounting symbol which served as a measure of comparison and indebtedness, and had no objective quantitative existence; the store of value and medium of exchange functions of money were assumed to be discharged through an assets structure of which cash and bank balances were only a part. Second, the assets structure was assumed to include both financial

* The present analysis differs from earlier analyses by the present writer (A. T. K. Grant, *A Study of the Capital Market in Britain*, pages 16-52; and *The Machinery of Finance and the Management of Sterling*, pages 20-40) as well as from that of the *Radcliffe Report*, all of which use the concept of a comprehensive assets structure, by taking the argument beyond the point of determination of effective demand and output to that of the determination of the price level as well; this opens the way for an exposition which covers the interactions between changes in all three – demand, output, prices – which in their turn are an essential part of the determination process.

claims/liabilities and physical assets, on the ground that since a purchase of a physical asset was an alternative to the acquisition of a financial claim (or for that matter of a bank balance) there was no ground for restricting the concept of assets. Third, a distinction was drawn between *ultimate* capacity to meet obligations, and the capacity to meet them on time *as they fell due*. It was on this latter basis – payments met as they fell due – that the taut structure of our financial arrangements depended, with its emphasis on liquidity as capacity to meet maturing obligations. Fourth, while the assumption on which the analysis was based started from a general equilibrium free market choice in the allocation of spending and in the acquisition of assets, the concept of government intervention was introduced; in particular, government as a voluntary participant in the assets market through debt management activities (open market operations, funding and unfunding); fiscal policy, the variation of the extent which government added to or subtracted from effective demand by varying the balance between revenue and expenditure through its capacity to impose or relieve obligation unilaterally; direct action in respect of financial institutions, not only by the creation or modification of such institutions, but also by the regulation of their working, such as by varying reserve ratios, or the rules under which they operate. Fifth, the further assumption was introduced that just as government could intervene to obligations unilaterally, so other organised interests could in certain circumstances impose charges (or the equivalent) which affected in varying degrees spending power, output and the assets structure. The examples chosen were organised labour in some of its wage bargaining aspects and organised business in price fixing and restrictive practices; it was suggested that for analytical purposes these might be regarded as equivalent to taxation. Sixth, given the facts that acts of intervention whether by government or by other bodies were not insulated in their effects but had repercussions, it was argued that certain policies, on the face of them reasonable, if pushed beyond a certain point had reverse effects: for example, increased taxation to prevent demand accelerating the rise in prices could beyond a certain point increase that rise in prices by eliciting irresistible demands for wage increases. There were other examples of such reversal effects.

The central feature of the analytical structure set out here is the replacement of the concept of money (cash and active bank balances) by a flexible but integrated assets structure which can expand and contract (in response to the outcome of a conflict of forces) to accommodate not only changes in taxation but also other obligations imposed from outside. (Organised business and labour are the contemporary U.K. examples, but one suspects much from economic history could be let in by this back door). The outcome is an attempt to translate what is in effect strict Keynesian theoretical analysis into an applied explanation of what has been happening in the mixed enterprise economy with which we are familiar.

There remains however a final speculative question: how will the financial mechanism develop in a mixed enterprise economy as it both gets richer and wealth is more widely spread.

Finance of its nature is a constraint which serves to apportion resources which are in limited supply. A modern financial system, as it evolves or is created, serves two distinct purposes. As an organisation it differentiates and classifies financial transactions, gives them recognisable shape, makes them easy to handle, brings together borrowers and lenders on a known basis, brings accepted techniques to bear to solve common problems. In doing these things it is widening and deepening the knowledge of productive activities which fit into the requirements of the economy; without it the input of materials and effort into producing would be slower and substantially less efficient because of more imperfect knowledge. In short, the same input would take longer or would result in a smaller output than is made possible by the greater knowledge of acceptable requirements which the system provides.

In its other purpose finance acts as a constraint: it imposes sense because ultimately it relates producers and consumers – and potential producers and consumers equally – on a realistic basis which sorts out priorities, and it does this because the basis of fulfilment of financial obligations is *settlement at due date*. What are the chances – and the consequences – of this basis becoming eroded if we all become wealthier, and moved from a liquidity to a net wealth basis?

If a large part of the community had appreciable possessions the loss of a substantial part of which would be inconvenient but would not be personally disastrous, borrowing capacity would be vastly increased; if things did not turn out as had been hoped, debtors could still be made to pay, and in the end there would be enough to compensate the creditor for the delay and the actuarial risk of insuring against absolute loss. Where a lot of rich people are concerned, the financial sanction would become an inconvenience rather than a constraint. Could such an erosion of finance as a constraint lead to a general instability in effective demand? If so, could not general instability become equated with general uncontrollability.

How much richer can you get?

The standard of living doubles in 35 years with real income per head growing at the rate of 2 per cent per annum continuously. In just under 24 years at 3 per cent. It doubles in 18 years at 4 per cent.

Put another way: assuming a working life of fifty years, someone starting work today will see a standard of living 2·7 times as high as now when he retires, with 2 per cent growth. With 3 per cent, $4\frac{1}{2}$ times. With 4 per cent, $7\frac{1}{2}$ times.

That is the measure of possibility – not of certainty – of increasing wealth.

This question comes up from another angle also. Economics is concerned with limited resources, though the word often used is 'scarcity', a misleadingly emotive word since real scarcity is dealt with not by the pricing system but by rationing. But the problem which emerges is this: limited resources can with increasing wealth become less scarce, less limited *in general* in relation to human needs. Put in another way, the general predictability to which the economic system is geared becomes less clearly marked, more capricious. So on the supply side we have greater uncertainty too.

What is the outcome in the community where greater wealth leads both to greater instability in effective demand and to greater uncertainty in the directions in which output is likely to be required? What in particular – to revert to present pre-occupations – happens to the movements of the price level, which may be increasingly subject to outside forces and which – as the argument here maintains – is precariously balanced with no automatic stabilisers to give it continuous support?

It could be that the balance of our mixed enterprise economy

– a large measure of free enterprise with active state participation and regulation where free enterprise is manifestly inadequate or inappropriate – will call for more direct and radical intervention from the state to give shape to economic processes which increasing affluence could make more incoherent.

Index